DEADLIER THAN THE MALE

IRELAND'S FEMALE
KILLERS

DEADLIER THAN THE MALE

IRELAND'S FEMALE
KILLERS

DAVID M KIELY

Gill & Macmillan

Gill & Macmillan Ltd
Hume Avenue, Park West, Dublin 12
with associated companies throughout the world
www.gillmacmillan.ie

© David M Kiely, 2005
0 7171 3894 1

Typography design by Make Communication
Print origination by TypeIT, Dublin
Printed by Nørhaven Paperback A/S, Denmark

This book is typeset in 10 on 12.5 pt Linotype Minion and
Neue Helvetica.

A CIP catalogue record for this book is available from the
British Library.

5 4 3 2 1

For McKenna,
as ever

CONTENTS

PREFACE

Practically from the first day *Bloody Women* appeared in the bookshops, in the autumn of 1999, readers have been lamenting my omissions. Why did I include the one murder and not the other? Didn't I know about Mrs A, who murdered her husband at about the same time as the O'Learys were slaughtering their brother? Or why I considered Fanny Barber's case more important than Mrs B's when they were so similar. And was I unaware of the notorious Mrs C and her murdering ways?

The simple answer is 'space'. My editor, Fergal Tobin, restricted me to 'between fifteen and twenty' murder cases, and we finally settled on seventeen. This new collection contains sixteen more, and begins roughly where *Bloody Women* began: the late nineteenth century. It also extends into the twenty-first, the final case being tried in 2004.

Few of us can doubt that Ireland, north and south, has become more violent in recent years. We seem to be keeping apace of a worldwide phenomenon, a dismaying trend that sees not only men but women and children kill with ever-increasing frequency.

We have child warriors—Amnesty International supplies us with the frightening statistic of 300,000 boy and girl soldiers fighting alongside their elders.

We have female suicide bombers. Not many, to be sure, but enough to sow terror among their intended victims. In September 2004 we witnessed something truly horrifying, and for most of us utterly unfathomable: women in a former Soviet state holding little children hostage with bombs.

Yet the astute reader will note that such women and children do not kill out of malice. There are stories behind the headlines. The guerrilla fighters may well be drafted into doing another's dirty work. They might have been pushed to the limit. A Palestinian woman may have seen her family wiped out in an Israeli rocket attack. A Chechen girl may have lost her parents to Russian brutality.

———

In the 1980s, Ireland was beginning to come of age. Long seen as the poorer relation of Britain and a source of cheap labour, the nation was turning the tables. The Celtic tiger was starting to flex its claws and growl.

But if the nation had grown up in an economic sense, its escalating crime showed that emotional growth was not keeping abreast. Particularly in the area of domestic violence—legal shorthand for wife-beating and rape within the home. It doesn't take a psychologist to decide that a man guilty of such crimes hasn't grown up, and that a society that looks with leniency on these crimes hasn't matured much either. A quick survey of the sentences meted out to husbands and partners who batter their women, sometimes over many years, brings one to the disquieting conclusion that the Irish courts haven't yet come to terms with the gravity of such crimes. Often a man found guilty of burglary is sent down for a longer term than a man found guilty of battering his wife almost to the point of death.

The prognosis is not good. The Women's Crisis Centre (WCC) recently published a disturbing statistic: that an estimated 42 per cent of Irishwomen were the victims of abuse, either in childhood or adulthood—or both. Given that many victims are extremely reluctant to come forward, even to the WCC, we can state with near-certainty that half the women of Ireland have been physically abused, assaulted or raped at one time or other in their lives.

———

It might be thought that because women were so often the victims of abuse then they themselves would go on to abuse others. This is, after all, a pattern that emerges time and again when we delve into the backgrounds of male murderers. Peter Sutcliffe, the 'Yorkshire Ripper', Geoffrey Daemer and Fred West were all abused in childhood. It's significant that we find fewer women turning the tables on their abusers or 'taking revenge' on others for the abuse they themselves suffered.

Domestic violence is a thread running through a great many of the cases you're about to read. Often the woman concerned felt she could take no more, that murder was her only means of escape from an abusive relationship.

It would, however, be foolish and indeed false to state that all the women at the centre of the following murder cases were free of guilt. Almost to a woman all were found guilty by juries, even if all were not sentenced accordingly.

———

How violent and cruel can women be? Given the right circumstances and motive, women can be vicious in the extreme. Rudyard Kipling wrote:

When the early Jesuit fathers preached to Hurons and Choctaws,
They prayed to be delivered from the vengeance of the squaws.
'Twas the women, not the warriors, turned those stark
enthusiasts pale.
For the female of the species is more deadly than the male.

Kipling was referring to the sadism of the 'squaws' who were known to reserve their most exquisite tortures for the prisoners delivered to them by their menfolk.

And not only the Choctaws and Hurons (or more properly the Wyandot). Many Native American nations conducted all-night torture rituals as acts of mourning, in which the women played the key roles. So feared were those sadistic women that men wounded in battle would unhesitatingly choose suicide rather than fall into their hands.

They were, we hope, the most extreme examples of female cruelty. The following pages will show that Ireland's women have never been strangers to murder.

———

Deadlier than the Male would not be the book it is were it not for the assistance and encouragement I received during its preparation. My thanks to all who shared their private lives and memories with me. My thanks to all those who helped in some small way or another (you know who you are). My special thanks to author Allen Foster for his tremendous help with researching a number of cases; a special mention too of Declan Higgins; and of writers Richard Clark, the late Eamon Collins, Brian Feeney, Seamus Kelters, David McKittrick and Chris Thornton, whose published work was invaluable to me.

David M Kiely
Rostrevor, February 2005

CATHERINE CLIFFORD AND THE RING OF POISONERS

Arsenic
Serves one

Ingredients
Six lengths of good quality flypaper
Salt, sugar or honey

Method
Boil the flypaper in a saucepan for 2–3 hours
Drain the juice and discard the paper
Let stand for 4–6 hours, depending on room temperature
When dry, remove the arsenic powder
Sprinkle with salt or sugar to taste
Serve 2–3 times a day in small doses, until death intervenes

In anyone's book it was an ingenious method of murder. Even more astonishing is the fact that the murderer was an uneducated, illiterate woman brought up in the slums of Liverpool. More astonishing still is that Catherine Flanagan might have gone on to dispose of scores more unfortunates—had the brother of her final victim not chanced by.

Catherine and her sister Margaret were first-generation Liverpool Irish. They hailed from County Wexford and had come to the city in 1849, their parents being desperate to escape the famine that raged in Ireland at the time. Liverpool was thriving. It had enjoyed its heyday in the eighteenth century when the slave trade generated immense wealth for those unscrupulous enough to pursue it. The despicable traffic in human beings was finally abolished in 1807 but Liverpool was undeterred. The traffic in human beings continued, but with a difference: now the ships carried legitimate, fare-paying passengers. Successive wars and revolutions had created in Europe a vast population of displaced persons, relatively speaking as many as the number of refugees in our time, including those seeking political asylum in more prosperous and welcoming lands. Liverpool became the hub from which those 'huddled masses' radiated out into the unknown.

Some wished to travel to America, others to Australia. There were thousands of Irish among them, many choosing to remain in the city rather than risk the long ocean voyage. Given what we know today about the 'coffin ships' that plied the Atlantic throughout the famine years we can appreciate the wisdom of this decision.

Yet the huge influx of Irish immigrants had to be housed, and slum after slum went up behind Liverpool's docklands and beyond. Just how bad some of those areas were can be deduced from contemporary accounts, which speak of families bringing up children in conditions that would have made even Charles Dickens blench. One of the slums was in Ascot Street. It lies in Everton, with Bootle to the north and the city centre to the south. Nowadays the traffic of two major roads separates the street from the docks a little to the west. The slum is long gone and on the site of Ascot Street stands a modest terrace of three-storey dwellings, most let out as flats for Liverpool's Asian community.

On a blustery day at the beginning of October 1883, Patrick Higgins decided to call on his brother Tom. A loan of one shilling and fourpence was long outstanding and Patrick, a docker, was not wealthy. On arriving at number 27 he heard a commotion coming from the basement flat where his brother lived. There were women's voices raised in song, and uncouth laughter.

Patrick went down the steps and pushed open the door. An incredible scene greeted him and he could hardly believe his eyes. The basement flat, filthy beyond words and lit only by a single oil lamp, seemed to be full of women—young, old and middle-aged. All were drunk, several so intoxicated that they could barely stand; it appeared to be a celebration of sorts. Patrick's astonishment turned to horror, however, when he saw what it was the women were celebrating. Lying in a rough coffin was his brother Tom, a man who just weeks before was in rude good health. Only thirty-six years of age, he had been a hod carrier in the building trade, a man so strong and able that his workmates had nicknamed him 'Crack-o'-the-Whip'.

At Patrick's appearance in the basement the women cut short their drunken revels. One of them appeared to sober up at once. It was Tom's wife: Margaret Higgins, *née* Clifford.

'He's after dying on us,' she told her brother-in-law sheepishly. 'It was the dysentery, according to Dr Whitford. You can ask him yourself.'

'I will,' said Patrick and stormed out, greatly distraught by the sight of his brother's corpse. Something was amiss.

The doctor in question had his practice near Bootle. Patrick went to him, was received without delay, and described what he'd seen. Dr Whitford confessed to having had no suspicions, yet agreed that a post-mortem might be useful.

'You'll have to arrange it quick, so, doctor,' Patrick said. 'They'll be putting my poor brother in his grave tomorrow.'

Whitford agreed and embarked at once on the necessary legal arrangements. He foresaw little difficulty in obtaining permission for the autopsy, he being a respected physician and on most agreeable terms with the coroner. Patrick in the meantime was returning home, his mind full of disquieting thoughts. He was remembering a rumour he'd heard not long before and was beginning to believe that there might be some truth in it after all.

The rumour doing the rounds of Liverpool's poorer quarters had it that men's lives were being insured without their knowledge. And the dismaying part was that it was very, very easy for the perpetrators. All one needed to do was to have someone pose as the victim and present himself at the offices of an insurance company. In a time when passports and driving licences belonged to the future, the birth record was virtually the sole proof of one's identity. More often than not, though, a busy insurance clerk had neither the time nor inclination to examine even this. In effect, then, a man could walk in off the street, claim he was somebody else, tender a small sum and have 'his' life insured for a far greater sum. It was that simple.

Patrick's fears were confirmed. More than that—matters proved to be far worse than he'd imagined. He visited as many insurance firms as he could in an afternoon, and found that no fewer than four had accepted premiums on his brother's life. Taken together they would pay out £108 on Tom's death. It was unlikely that Tom when alive had even *seen* such a large sum. Patrick suspected who it was who'd stand to gain from his brother's untimely demise.

He took a cab posthaste to Bootle and found that Dr Whitford had already obtained permission to examine the corpse. Suspecting that they might meet with opposition from the widow and the other women, the two enlisted the services of a police constable.

They arrived at 27 Ascot Street not a moment too soon. A hearse stood outside and the undertaker and his assistant were making ready to depart with the remains, watched with interest by Catherine Flanagan, the widow's sister—and three other women, all dressed in their Sunday clothes—and each seeming to have once again indulged in the demon drink. The doctor held up a hand.

'The coroner has ordered a post-mortem,' he announced. 'The funeral cannot take place today.'

It was a good thing that a constable had accompanied them because Catherine at once launched a torrent of invective. She was joined by the widow, Margaret, who flew at Patrick Higgins, screaming obscenities. The other women barred the way to the coffin. The constable drew his truncheon and advanced—leaving the front door unguarded.

'Away with you now, Catherine!' a woman shouted. 'Get away now or they'll hang you.'

But Catherine Flanagan, despite her stocky build and long skirts, was already on the steps and mounting them as fast as she could. As Patrick extricated himself from Margaret Higgins and the constable reached for his whistle she was halfway down Ascot Street, to disappear in Liverpool's docklands.

Margaret had made no attempt to flee. It was to prove a mistake because the post-mortem revealed that Thomas Higgins had died not of dysentery but of arsenic poisoning. Margaret was arrested and held in custody pending the apprehension of her sister.

There followed a police investigation that some said was long overdue. It threw up some dismaying facts. It revealed the existence of a crime syndicate that overturned the notion that organized crime was the bailiwick of the male. More, it showed Catherine and Margaret Clifford to be two of the most heartless and unscrupulous murderers Ireland had ever produced. Even now, more than a century on, we have yet to uncover the full extent of their crimes. We can reconstruct most of them, however, thanks to the work of retired solicitor Angela Brabin, who published her findings in *History Today*. Her superb forensic research makes for chilling reading as she pieces together the story of the Clifford sisters and their nefarious careers. She discovered that they were not operating alone, that there were other women involved—perhaps those who'd gathered in Ascot Street on that bleak October morning to toast the success of yet another well-laid scheme of murder.

———

It began in 1881 when Thomas Higgins, his wife and ten-year-old daughter Mary took lodgings in Skirving Street, Everton, at the home of Mrs Catherine Flanagan. She was a widow. Dark rumours that circulated in the district suggested that her widowhood was of her own making, but we must discount the rumours and examine only the facts—Catherine's subsequent and well-documented misdeeds are evidence enough of her wickedness. At forty-seven she was not an attractive woman. Her face was scarred in several places and a number of teeth were missing, all the results of beatings she'd endured at the hands of an abusive husband, a Dublin-born docker. Nor was she friendly: her dark eyes and large gold earrings had an unsettling effect on those meeting her for the first time. In her defence we must conclude that she'd been brutalized by her past, and that the lure of easy money was strong for one who'd known grinding poverty for such a long time.

Within weeks Mrs Higgins was dead. It would be wrong to suspect foul play because again we have no evidence, yet Thomas did remarry with seemingly undue haste—in October of the same year—and the bride was Catherine's sister Margaret. She was an attractive woman, not yet forty at the time, with a gentle demeanour that Thomas found irresistible. The fact that his daughter Mary took an instant dislike to her stepmother should perhaps have set him thinking.

Margaret was herself a widow, whose husband had been taken by dysentery some three months before the arrival in Skirving Street of Thomas Higgins and family. Catherine's husband had died of the same illness the previous year. It could be argued that the insanitary conditions in which these slum-dwellers lived invited such deaths, yet some felt that it was highly suspect when little Mary Higgins died within a month of her father's marriage to Margaret Clifford. The cause? Consumption. And ten months before, in December 1880, Catherine Clifford's son John had succumbed to the same disease when only twenty-two.

Neighbours had noted that Catherine had appeared less the grieving mother than one might have expected, and seemed indecently pleased with the life-insurance payment she'd received. It amounted to £71—the equivalent of several thousand pounds in today's money. It was indeed a sum to crow about: in life the luckless young man's labouring job paid less than £10 a year.

And in January 1883, under Thomas Higgins's very nose, yet

another untimely death occurred at 27 Ascot Street, the sisters' new home. This time the deceased was Maggie Jennings, an eighteen-year-old and the daughter of one of Catherine's lodgers, a man with whom Catherine had been having sexual relations. Catherine did well from the girl's death too: it brought her £79.

By the time she fled from the authorities she was a wealthy woman.

——

The hunt was on. The Liverpool police issued handbills with the fugitive's description. 'Mrs Flanagan', they read, 'is about 50 years of age, 5ft 2ins in height, stout build, full features, fresh complexion, freckled face, dark eyes . . . and speaks with a strong Irish accent.'

From Margaret they'd learned that the sisters had an uncle—Thomas Clifford—living in Dumfries, Scotland. It was assumed she'd head north to see him, and possibly make her way to America where she had friends and family.

But Catherine had made no contingency plans, had not considered the possibility that she'd be found out. Her successes had made her arrogant. Now she was running for her life—and she could not doubt that arrest would lead to the gallows. She hurried to Rockingham Street, no more than a stone's throw from her home, and rapped on the door of number four. Mrs Mackenzie knew the fugitive to see, though not by name—Catherine was well known in the district—and had spoken to her once when her husband had met with an accident; it seemed to Mrs Mackenzie that she had a sympathetic ear.

Catherine was now calling on the neighbour to return the kindness. She needed to lie low, she said. Her son was looking for her, she explained, in a gush of words. Mrs Mackenzie smelled drink—a great deal of it.

'You better come in then,' she said.

The fugitive, when she'd got her breath, went on to say that she'd come into a sum of money—'seven pounds and some odd shillings'—paid to her by a club. It was one of many savings schemes run by the poor of Liverpool in a time that predated the credit unions, though the working folk of Rochdale had been toying with the idea of a credit union for a number of years. Catherine asked if she could stay the night. Her intention was to disappear to Scotland, where her son John was unlikely to pursue her. She seemed to Mrs Mackenzie to be in great fear of the young man, and the neighbour recalled that he did indeed have a fearsome reputation for violence when he'd 'drink taken'. She assured her visitor that she could stay as long as she wished.

In the event, Catherine remained with the kindly neighbour for four days, departing on the Tuesday. Before she left she begged of Mrs Mackenzie one last favour. Handing her a penny she asked if she wouldn't mind buying a copy of the *Liverpool Echo*. The neighbour obliged and returned shortly with the paper.

'Is there anything in there about John McCormack?' Catherine asked, and it was only then that her benefactor realized that she was illiterate. She put on her spectacles. 'He's supposed to be tried today.'

Mrs Mackenzie assumed the man was Catherine's son. But there was nothing. She did, however, spot another news item, one that filled her with dismay.

'Oh dear me!' she exclaimed.

'What is it, what is it?' Catherine was agitated.

'It's the wholesale poisoning case.'

'Read it for me.'

Mrs Mackenzie's hands shook as she perused the small print.

'Oh, the walking devil!' she cried at last.

'Who?'

'Mrs Flanagan, that's who. She-devil that she is! I could find it in my heart to string her up myself.'

Catherine sensed that the game was up, that her sister Margaret had broken under questioning and confessed to her part in the villainous activities in Ascot Street. As the kindly neighbour read aloud from the paper, Catherine heard that she too had been implicated—or at any rate a sister of the woman in police custody. The report carried a summary description of the suspect but it was vague. Mrs Mackenzie seemed not to suspect a thing. The authorities were searching for a Mrs Flanagan, wanted for murder, and the good lady was giving refuge to a Mrs Clifford, in hiding from a violent son. She'd no call to make the connection.

But *somebody* evidently knew where Catherine was holed up, and this part of the story has never been adequately explained. At some time between the Thursday and the following Tuesday the fugitive must have slipped out of the house and alerted friends to her whereabouts because that evening she received two male visitors looking for 'Catherine'.

'Hurry up and get your bonnet and shawl on,' one urged. 'I want to speak to you outside.'

'Why don't you and Mrs Clifford go up to the parlour and talk there,' Mrs Mackenzie suggested.

They complied. Some minutes later, however, Catherine came down again to the kitchen. She seemed greatly perturbed.

'He's gone,' she said simply.

'Who's gone?'

'My son.'

She said it with a leaden voice. Now Mrs Mackenzie thought to understand the visit by the two men. The son was dead.

'God help you,' she said. 'God rest his soul.'

'No, no,' Catherine said, 'you misunderstand. It's not dead he is but in gaol. I'm going to have to go and see him.'

'Of course, dear,' agreed Mrs Mackenzie, and helped Catherine to pack a few things she very generously gave her, along with a half-crown. Shortly afterwards the fugitive left with the two men, and her benefactor never saw her alive again.

———

On the morning of 10 October 1883, a week following Tom Higgins's death, a guesthouse owner in Mount Vernon Street, Bootle, answered her door to a woman seeking lodgings. Mrs Clifford explained that she'd just arrived from Manchester and needed a base from which to conduct a mission of mercy.

'It's my niece,' she explained to Mrs Booth over a cup of tea in the parlour. 'They're after putting her in the workhouse and I'm here to get her out of there.'

'Oh.'

'I'm all she has, you see,' the visitor explained. 'The father ran off and the mother passed away last February.'

Mrs Booth gave Catherine a room for a week—'or longer if you need it'—and left her lodger to her own devices. She noticed, however, that Mrs Clifford made no attempt to rescue her niece during her stay, but remained in the house, complaining of rheumatism. It was a cold October that particular year and Mrs Clifford seemed to be genuinely suffering. Mrs Booth 'nursed and coddled' her new lodger, administering hot soup and keeping the fire going in Catherine's room. The days passed. The hue and cry subsided.

On the Friday, Catherine requested a newspaper and Mrs Booth obliged. With her lodger propped up in her warm bed and a nice cup of tea to hand, she read aloud the local news. The search for the poisoner was still on, though the police were no longer making of it a priority.

'Tell me,' Catherine said, 'what do you think of this Mrs Flanagan?'

'A fiend in human form!' Mrs Booth replied without hesitation. 'A she-devil,' she added, echoing Mrs Mackenzie's words.

Catherine nodded.

'Do you think she'll be caught? It's a while now, so it is.'

'Oh, they'll catch her all right,' Mrs Booth said with conviction. 'The police always catch them in the end. Crime doesn't pay.'

Saturday's *Echo* carried more news. The results of the inquest into the death of Thomas Higgins revealed that he'd died of arsenic poisoning.

'It's shocking,' Mrs Booth said. 'The poor man, how he must have suffered! I hope they hang the pair of them.'

'They will,' said Catherine.

'Speaking of hanging,' Mrs Booth continued cheerfully, 'did you hear that old Willie Marwood is retiring?'

'The executioner?'

'The very one. The Gentle Executioner they call him. He'll be missed too. He always treated his guests well, no matter how black-hearted they were. I suppose there's something to be said for that sort of Christian consideration.'

Catherine was thoughtful as she sipped her tea. 'Who do you think will get the job now?' she asked.

'They say it could be Bartholomew Binns. But they do say he's a terrible bungler. Drunk every day of his life. Half the time he doesn't know what he's doing.'

Catherine had heard the stories. Marwood became public hangman in 1874 when he took over from William Calcraft. The latter was not the most careful of executioners, generally giving his victims the 'short drop', what amounted in effect to slow strangulation, an extremely painful death. Marwood was to insist on a drop that broke the neck of the condemned. Death was swift and relatively painless. But Binns, Catherine knew, would have no such scruples. Did her teacup rattle on its saucer as she contemplated a messy and agonizing end at the hands of a drunkard? No doubt it did.

In any event Catherine was determined to remain one step ahead of the law. She might be recognized at any time, perhaps by one of Mrs Booth's other lodgers. She therefore paid her bill the following Monday—from a 'purse full of gold', which aroused the landlady's suspicions. She remembered her lodger's stated reasons for visiting the city: the mission of mercy to the workhouse. Catherine informed her that she was going to see her niece that very day.

'I'll come with you if you like,' said Mrs Booth. 'I'd like to see the poor girl.'

'I doubt if she'd like to see you!' Catherine snapped, causing the landlady to wonder whom it was she'd had under her roof for a week or more. But they parted amicably and Catherine made her way on foot to Wavertree. She'd decided that it was safer to board a train for Scotland in this quiet suburb where it was unlikely that the authorities were on the alert. She stopped to look in on Mrs McGovern, a fellow Irishwoman in the curiously named One Street, and settled down to a cup of tea and a chat.

She was due to leave Liverpool that night; her intention was to board a train to Blackburn and continue on to Scotland the following day. As a 'going-away treat' she invited Mrs McGovern to join her for a drink at the Station Hotel in Wellington Street. It was to be Catherine's biggest mistake.

One drink led to many more and before long she was drunk and loose-tongued, buying rounds for the hangers-on in the hotel lounge.

'I'm on the run, you know,' she boasted. 'The bobbies are looking for me.'

Her audience assumed she was joking but there was no stopping Catherine. She related how she'd made off with furniture belonging to her son and was being pursued by the police. It was nonsense, of course, yet contained one significant item of truth—Catherine named Ascot Street as the scene of the crime.

Unknown to the poisoner the police had offered a reward for information leading to her capture, and an individual at the bar pricked up his ears. He remembered a description of Mrs Catherine Flanagan he'd read on a handbill, saw how this woman's scars and missing teeth fitted with that description, and left the company unnoticed. Minutes later he was confiding his suspicions to Inspector Keighley and Sergeant Hill, men who were delighted that the infamous Irishwoman sought by their colleagues in the metropolitan police had drifted into their jurisdiction. They hurried to the hotel, but Catherine and her friend had already left, to return to One Street.

Mrs McGovern was giving lunch when the detectives arrived. Catherine, though shocked initially, recovered herself and replied calmly to the questions. No, she insisted, she didn't know what they were talking about. She'd come down from Blackburn the day before to visit her friend and would be returning that night.

'And you say your name is Clifford?' Keighley asked. She nodded.

The name had set him thinking. He was remembering the wording of the official police wanted poster. 'Mrs Flanagan', it read, 'has an uncle named Thomas Clifford, residing at 10 Burns

Street, Dumfries, Scotland. She will no doubt endeavour to leave the country, having friends in America.' Everything fitted, even the big hooped earrings the suspect still wore.

'I am taking you into custody,' he told her, 'as Catherine Flanagan, wanted on suspicion of murder.'

'I know nothing about that!' she cried defiantly. But she knew she was cornered, and even before they reached the station she was admitting her identity. She might well be Catherine Flanagan, she said, but she was no murderer.

'It's not right what they're saying about me in the papers. It's not right.'

Few were going to believe her, though, and when word of her arrest spread—and it spread exceedingly fast—a mob gathered to boo and denounce her as she was escorted into the station. There were loud cries of 'Poisoner!' and 'Villain!' and men pressed forward to compliment the police on the apprehension of the 'she-devil'.

Catherine's guilt was never going to be in doubt. She could but hope for mitigation, and to this end tried to come to an arrangement with the prosecutor. She offered to testify against her sister Margaret but heard that her testimony would make little difference. The police had found all the evidence they needed in the basement flat in Ascot Street.

They discovered what amounted to a small factory for the production of arsenic. There were the remains of flypaper, and the strips had clearly been boiled. There was the very pot that had been used for the extraction process—and a foul-smelling solution in the bottom of the pot was found to contain arsenic. Most damning of all was a quantity of the deadly toxin found in one of Margaret's pockets.

And there were the bodies. That of Margaret's husband contained more than enough arsenic to kill him, but the police went further. They procured exhumation orders and dug up the corpses of three more victims: those of Catherine's son John, Thomas Higgins's daughter Mary, and Maggie Jennings, the eighteen-year-old daughter of Catherine's erstwhile lover. All contained lethal quantities of arsenic. Allowing for contamination by the soil surrounding the interred remains, the amounts tallied roughly with those found in Thomas Higgins's body.

No one but the Clifford sisters could have administered the poison. The investigators heard that in Higgins's case only Catherine and Margaret had been present towards the end, giving them ample time and opportunity to do the deed. They'd been unusually clever too, the police learned. In each case they waited until a *bona fide* illness had laid the victim low—in each instance an upset stomach or bowel disorder. In those less hygiene-conscious times it was not uncommon for a mild ailment like heartburn to develop into something more life threatening. The sisters were on hand to ensure that it did just that.

By anyone's standards it was a cruel death, an end one might conceivably wish upon one's worst enemy but not on an innocent family member—in Catherine's case her very own son. The police reconstructed how the women had set to work.

It's notoriously difficult to administer the correct dose of arsenic. Use too much and the victim dies immediately; too small a dose given over a period of days (or weeks) may have no more effect than a mouldy shortcake biscuit. The body can build up a tolerance for arsenic. Used in small quantities it can even improve the complexion and help reduce weight, though few dieticians would dream of prescribing it. Used as poison in the correct dose it saps the victim's strength, causing purging and vomiting—and excruciating pain. It seems odd that the physicians called in to examine the sisters' victims should not have recognized the symptoms. We can only conclude that the poisoners began using the arsenic *after* the doctor had diagnosed an ostensibly harmless ailment. Dr Whitford, the man who drew up the death certificate on Thomas Higgins's death, had given dysentery as the cause of death. Considering the filthy state of the basement flat where Higgins had lain, he would not have been surprised that the disease had carried off the luckless labourer. 'Death by dirt' would have done just as well.

Catherine managed to pull the wool over another doctor's eyes. When the lodger Maggie Jennings was ill she called in a Dr Rafter, pretending to be the girl's mother. She showed him some blood that Maggie had brought up and the doctor diagnosed pneumonia. Catherine carefully withheld mention of her other symptoms, and when asked about the girl's bowel movements replied that they were regular. Maggie's father was likewise kept in the dark. In hindsight it was all so incredibly easy.

———

When the sisters were led into the dock together in February 1884 the courtroom was full to bursting. So great was the venom unleashed from the visitors' gallery that the judge had to clear the court twice before the proceedings could get underway.

The trial lasted three days. A succession of witnesses appeared and, as the trial progressed, revealed a shocking conspiracy on the part of the Clifford sisters. They also brought to light the incredible laxness that typified the insurance companies of the time. The firms relied a little too much on their agents, who were paid commission on the life insurance they sold. One such agent, George Griffith, told how Scottish Legal routinely paid him the value of the first eight weeks' premiums, and thereafter a twenty-five per cent commission. It was a lucrative business, open to exploitation. Insurance premium collectors told the court that it was customary to allow wives to sign for their husbands, and the judge listened in astonishment.

The court heard how Thomas Higgins almost discovered the tricks of his wife and sister-in-law. Giving evidence was Francis Dominic Bowles, district supervisor for the Pearl Life Assurance Company, whose testimony went some way to explain how the Clifford sisters operated. In March 1883 Margaret wished to add a further £40 to the sum at which her husband's life was insured. An agent filled in the relevant form, Margaret paid the premium, and all seemed well. Until Supervisor Bowles visited the house in Ascot Street to see the insured in person.

The sisters panicked. To produce Thomas himself was out of the question; he was unaware that his life was insured—by more than one company. For the price of a pint of porter a neighbour was persuaded to impersonate Thomas. The supervisor was satisfied that 'Mr Higgins' was in excellent health and therefore a good insurance risk, and a medical certificate was duly signed.

But Francis Bowles was thorough. On learning of Thomas's death in October he visited the house in person to secure the widow's signature on the claim form. As the illiterate Margaret was making her mark Bowles happened to glance at the corpse, and was bemused to see that the man in the coffin bore no resemblance to the person he'd vetted that same spring. He snatched back the paper, muttered something about 'formalities' and left the house, intending to go to the authorities. As it turned out, they came to him instead.

Had the prosecutors wished to do so then they could easily have extended the proceedings to include other women in the area of Ascot Street, and the testimony of more than one witness hinted that the Clifford sisters were part of a wider crime ring, that there was a veritable poisoning 'industry' at work in the slums of Liverpool, that no one was truly safe when it was so easy to insure the life of another without his or her knowledge. Supervisor Bowles was exceptional—very few checks were made, even by the most reputable of companies. The suspicion grew that the four deaths attributed to the Cliffords were simply the most recent in a long history of arsenic murders. What, the judge wondered, had become of Catherine's husband? And a number of lodgers who'd died supposedly of natural causes in Sterling Street?

Four murders were enough, however, to condemn Catherine and her sister. They were to hang, together, on 3 March 1884.

Some days prior to the execution the dread news arrived: Bartholomew Binns—'Botcher' Binns—was to dispatch the sisters. Many in Liverpool saw in this choice a grim justice of sorts, and hoped that Binns might be drunk enough to reward the two poisoners with a slow and agonizing end. Had they not sat quietly by while their innocent victims suffered excruciating pain for days on end?

As it turned out, their end was mercifully swift. Binns had

brought with him an assistant hangman, one who—to quote the wry comment made by a journalist of the time—'knew the ropes'. As a late fall of snow lay in the yard of Kirkdale Gaol, Catherine and Margaret Clifford were positioned side by side beneath the gallows beam, the trap was sprung and they dropped almost to the ground. Death, reported the physicians on hand, was practically instantaneous.

BELLINA PRIOR AND THE INFANT IN THE BOILER

Bellina Prior was insane. In our day her mental illness might have been diagnosed as schizophrenia. We might even have been able to discover the root cause, whether it was a result of a childhood trauma or it 'ran in the family'. She might be treated with narcotics that suppressed the symptoms and allowed her to lead a useful life. She might not be cured but she wouldn't be allowed to suffer either. And crucially, those around her would be safeguarded from the delusions created by her disturbed mind.

But this was Armagh in 1888. Bellina enjoyed little sympathy and understanding in a time when mental illness was still called lunacy—literally an ailment brought about by overexposure to the rays of the moon. Mental hospitals were still referred to as 'bedlam', a word arrived at from Bethlehem, the name given to the most notorious asylum of them all: that run by St Bartholomew's in London. It was a fearsome place. The mother of nineteen-year-old Bellina would remember easily when its occupants were kept in chains as in a freak show, and visitors were charged a penny to see them. A Royal Commission was to change all that in 1851 but in Armagh city mental illness was still feared and loathed. You didn't speak about an unstable relative or sibling; all was kept behind closed doors.

Bellina's family had more reason than most to keep quiet about her fits and attacks. They were people of high standing in the city. Her father, Colonel Charles Prior, who died when she was still a child, had commanded the army garrison for a number of years. His widow, Nina, was regarded as one of the most upstanding members of the community and her other children—two boys, aged seventeen and fourteen, and a daughter, Adele, sixteen—were looked up to as models of propriety. All the same they lived in straitened circumstances—what you might call 'genteel poverty', getting by on Nina's widow's pension. On the colonel's death she'd had to sell the house to pay outstanding debts. Certain benefactors had interceded for her to acquire a house on Vicar's Hill, a row of fine granite dwellings built in the previous century to accommodate the widows of clergymen. The houses faced onto the grounds of St Patrick's, the magnificent and historic Church of Ireland cathedral, and the deafening peal of its bells had become a part of the children's daily life. The colonel's offspring fitted well into the little Protestant community of Vicar's Hill. No one in the street, or in the family's circle of friends, suspected that Bellina was a lethal danger to herself and those around her.

We do not know when the attacks began because Nina Prior wanted no one to know. We know only that some six weeks before the dreadful incident that took place on Tuesday, 27 March, Bellina was displaying a 'peculiar manner'. Her mother put it down to moodiness. The situation took a nasty turn, however, on 20 March. Bellina entered from the yard brandishing a hatchet, went into the drawing-room where Nina, son Harvey and daughter Adele were reading and writing letters, and attacked all three. Mother and son dodged the weapon but Adele wasn't quick enough. The hatchet caught her a glancing blow to the head. She was lucky to escape with her life. She managed to overpower Bellina and take the hatchet from her. Eventually the young woman calmed down and peace was restored.

Nina Prior noted that her daughter's fits were erratic and unpredictable. Days could go by when Bellina appeared normal. The fits would come unprovoked, her speech grow incoherent and there would be 'a wild look in her eye'. Following the incident with the hatchet Nina considered calling on the advice of the Reverend Benjamin Wade, a minister serving at the nearby cathedral and a family friend of long standing. Wade was a learned man, well read; apart from his ministry he was active in the upkeep of Armagh's excellent library. He'd also served as chaplain to a mental hospital and could have offered good counsel. But Nina said nothing; the good name of her family was more important than anything else.

And so it was that when a neighbour left a baby girl in the care of the Prior girls she could have no reason to think that she was placing her in mortal danger.

Kate Slevin was nine years old and a familiar face in the Prior household. She'd help out when needed—Nina Prior couldn't afford to employ servants—and occasionally run an errand for the family. She was a daughter of Joseph Slevin, a plasterer and whitewasher by trade.

Mrs Slevin was feeling unwell that Tuesday and took to her bed. She asked Kate if she'd mind looking after her youngest child, three-year-old Annie. Kate reminded her mother that she'd promised Nina Prior to help with the shopping that day—but yes, she could take Annie with her. The Prior girls would be happy to look after her for an hour or two.

All seemed in order when she arrived at the house on Vicar's Hill. The door was open and Nina Prior ready to leave. Bellina took little Annie by the hand and promised Kate she'd look after her sister. It was well known that Bellina adored children. Kate, if anything, feared that Bellina might spoil the child too much.

Indeed the first thing the girl did was bring Annie into the dining-room and give her sweets. It was two in the afternoon. Then Bellina announced to her sister Adele that she was going to the kitchen to bake a cake for the family tea that evening. She said she would bring the child along. Annie thought it was great fun.

Fifteen minutes went by. Bellina returned to the dining-room—alone.

'Where's Annie?' Adele asked casually. 'I thought she was with you.'

It was only then she noticed that Bellina's face was a deathly white. Her dress was soaking wet. Adele knew that something was terribly wrong.

'I didn't do it,' Bellina said, but she said it under her breath and Adele had difficulty understanding her.

'Do what?'

'I didn't do it,' Bellina repeated.

She sat down in a chair and buried her face in her hands. When she looked up again she was calmer.

'Very well,' she told her sister, 'I did do it. I've killed the child.'

Adele waited for nothing more but raced out of the room and down to the kitchen. For as long as she lived she never forgot the sight that met her eyes.

There was a large damp patch on the stone-flagged kitchen floor close to the cooking range. Beside the range was a big copper boiler. It was open, and Adele, to her horror, saw a pair of little sandalled feet protruding from it. She ran to the boiler and saw Annie Slevin half immersed in the cold water. She pulled her out but it was too late. The child was dead.

How had the child got into the boiler? Like the stove it was set into the masonry with its door at chest level—but at the level of an adult's chest. A child of three wouldn't have been able to clamber into it unaided. True, there was a chair nearby, and a number of large tin cans. Conceivably Annie could have climbed up onto a can and fallen into the boiler. But Adele found her lying on her back. Somebody had placed her there.

Adele hurried to the cathedral and summoned the beadle, the most trusted person she knew. She told him she had to get word immediately to her mother on the other side of the city. Within minutes he'd located her and Nina Prior returned home to Vicar's Hill around 4.30 pm. She learned the grim news. Although in a state of shock she had the presence of mind to go to the cathedral herself and search out Reverend Wade.

They went together to the house. By this time fourteen-year-old Harvey had come home from the Royal School and was trying to comfort Adele, who was nearly hysterical. He indicated that his sister Bellina could be found in the parlour. And no, he

hadn't alerted the authorities yet; he hoped that Reverend Wade could advise on that matter.

Wade found Bellina alone in the parlour, seemingly more composed than she had a right to be—certainly calmer than her mother and sister. She didn't seem surprised to see him or concerned at the graveness of his manner. Already he could detect the familiar signs of a disturbed mind.

'What is this you've done, Bellina?' he asked quietly.

She shook her head.

'I won't say a word,' she told him. She looked up as her mother entered. Wade thought to detect some tension between the two.

'Tell the Reverend Wade about it, Bellina,' Nina Prior coaxed.

Bellina maintained her silence for some time. Finally it seemed as though a weight were lifted from her, because she suddenly found her voice and rounded on her mother.

'Mother, I have paid you off,' she cried, 'and I'm glad of it!'

She sat down and stared at the floor.

'Everyone is unkind to me.'

'In what way, dear?' her mother asked gently, but Bellina lapsed into silence again. Wade reached down and took the girl's hand.

'Do you know what you've done?' he asked. 'Do you know that you've taken the life of that poor child?'

The accusation seemed to have a startling effect on Bellina. She looked up into Wade's eyes with an expression that he would later describe as 'maniacal'. He was shaken.

'Do you know what the consequences will be to yourself?' he asked.

'I'll be hanged I suppose,' she answered defiantly, 'and I'll be glad of it!'

The minister was shocked by the outburst. The seeming callousness of the girl disturbed him. She was smiling, as though she'd been accused of playing a practical joke. If he'd doubted before this that Bellina Prior's mind was unhinged then he was now convinced of it.

He had a quiet word with her mother and went to the police. He did so with great reluctance as he knew that incarceration would naturally follow. In his learned opinion a prison was the last place for Bellina to be. She needed medical attention, not the misery of a cell. Yet he knew that such a fate awaited the young woman. A child lay dead by her hand.

District-Inspector Bailey was a no-nonsense man. A crime was a crime as far as he was concerned. He knew the family well, had been a good friend of the late Colonel Prior, and was certainly no stranger to Bellina. But when he came to arrest her she acted as though she didn't know him at all, not even when he donned his official hat, as it were, and formally charged her with the murder of little Annie Slevin.

As is the case in large towns and small cities, word had got out long before the constabulary arrived at the house on Vicar's Hill. A small crowd had gathered by the time Bellina was escorted out onto the street. By evening all Armagh had learned of the dreadful tragedy. Mrs Slevin was inconsolable. No one had suspected that pretty little Bellina, a model of kindness, could commit such a callous and unprovoked crime.

The case first came up before a magistrate, an inquest was duly held, and the case tried in Armagh courthouse on 7 April. Bellina's family were sworn in, as were a number of neighbours and friends. As Bellina stood motionless in the dock, guarded by the matron of Armagh Gaol, and the evidence of all was heard, no one in the courtroom was left in any doubt that she had indeed wilfully and deliberately drowned the child in the boiler. There was no question of its being an accident. Annie couldn't have climbed in by herself; somebody had coldly and callously held her head under the water until her struggles had subsided. That somebody could only have been Bellina Prior.

Was she insane? Reverend Wade told the magistrate that in his opinion she was—or at the very least there was 'something mentally wrong with her'. The magistrate, Captain Prescott, RM, returned the case for trial.

Bellina appeared before Mr Justice Murphy on Wednesday, 12 July, by which time she'd languished in custody for more than four months. All could see that she'd suffered terribly and there were few in that court who felt no pity for her. Yet murder had been done and Bellina would have to pay. The judge determined that she'd 'wilfully, feloniously and of malice aforethought, killed and murdered' little Annie Slevin. He sentenced her to life imprisonment—a harsh sentence, though less than the customary one of death by hanging. The prisoner was taken down.

———

The tragedy didn't end there. They brought Bellina Prior to Armagh city gaol in a covered carriage that would discourage the nosiness of the prurient. Even when they locked her again in the grim but by now familiar cell, no one considered that in her unstable condition she might be a danger to herself. In our time Bellina would have been assigned a suicide watch. In the event she tried to kill herself by cutting her throat. Heavily bandaged and in great pain, she was taken to a lunatic asylum in Belfast.

If there were those who wondered what it was that had caused the nineteen-year-old to lose her mind then no comment was made at the time. Yet a vital clue can be found in the evidence given at the trial. It emerged that Nina Prior had a burning desire for Bellina to enter the acting profession. Her motives were money and fame; it was at a time when successful actors both in Ireland and Britain commanded sizeable salaries. Nina had followed closely the career of Ellen Terry and her wonderfully lucrative partnership with theatrical great Henry Irving. Nina had been a beauty at the time of her marriage. She may even have seen herself following in the footsteps of Ellen Terry, for whom Oscar Wilde once wrote a sonnet. It was a girlish dream that would never be realized. So she singled out her daughter Bellina—pretty, petite Bellina—to realize the dream for her.

'In a slow and subtle process,' notes a British psychologist, 'parents infuse into their children a psychological web which traps feelings and permits no release—an inner rigidity bucking against one's natural impulses.' If that child is unable to meet impossible expectations then anguish will ensue. The energy of that anguish and frustration 'will be added to the general pool of psychological pain, ultimately leading to overload. . . .'

Nina Prior's attempts to bend her daughter's will to hers turned an impossible dream into a nightmare, one that was to lead to the death of an innocent young child. It was a tragedy that claimed so many victims: Annie Slevin and her family, the heartbroken Nina Prior, and the person at the centre of the tragedy, Bellina Prior herself. Driven insane by her mother's demands, she died in a mental hospital, alone and forgotten, at the age of fifty-five.

HANNAH FLYNN AND THE MURDER OF THE FARMER'S WIFE

Mention Killorglin and first thoughts turn to Puck Fair. It's a modern extravaganza of good times and innocent excess riding on the back of an ancient pagan festival. Each year people flock to this little Kerry community from all parts of Ireland and abroad. The *craic* is good, the ladies are beautiful and the lads are up for a no-holds-barred fine time, all in honour of the goat king.

That is Kerry now. In April 1923 it was an altogether darker 'kingdom'. Civil war was tearing Ireland apart. If life wasn't exactly cheap then it wasn't highly valued either—that is, among the ranks of Free State forces and Irregulars who fought with ferocious savagery for control of the Twenty-Six Counties that had been wrested from Britain's grip of centuries.

It didn't augur well for the fledgling state. Everybody was to blame and nobody was to blame. Éamon de Valera's supporters blamed Michael Collins for having signed a flawed treaty and refused to recognize the state. Collins's Free State Army blamed the Irregulars for turning the country into a battlefield.

In more peaceful times the murder of Margaret O'Sullivan would have dismayed and horrified country folk the length and breadth of Kerry. As it was, the forty-year-old farmer's wife joined the list of casualties produced since 1919, meriting only the most summary reporting in the local press, and a line or two in the national newspapers. For on and about the day she died—Easter Sunday, 1 April—the civil war was in its death throes. April would see the arrest of de Valera and a cessation of hostilities, but hardliners were fighting on to the bitter end.

That same Easter weekend in Tipperary, in the Glen of Aherlow, Captain O'Dea of the Free State army and Jerry Kiely, a local militia leader, were gunned down as they defended a farmhouse that had come under attack by Irregulars. In County Louth an army barracks sustained heavy fire on Saturday night, with many wounded. Bombs were hurled at men guarding the power station in Cork city.

In Tullamore the Irregulars tried to blow up a bridge. Counties Limerick, Clare, Monaghan and Waterford all experienced fighting that erupted on Good Friday and lasted until Easter Sunday.

In County Kerry, in Caragh, a railway linesman was kidnapped on the Friday night. More sinister still was the finding of a man's body dumped on the Glenbeigh road, some three miles outside Killorglin. It was that of Michael O'Shea, a volunteer with Collins's forces. He'd been shot in the face and chest at point-blank range—an execution—and a mocking message from the Irregulars was hung around his neck.

And later that same day they found the body of Margaret O'Sullivan. It was, it seemed, in its own repulsive way, an execution as well. Whoever killed her had gone for the face, just like poor Michael O'Shea. The murderer must have hated her too because he'd mutilated her face so much that her own husband Daniel barely recognized her. Her skull had been bashed in. An inquest would show that she'd been struck eighteen times in all—perhaps sixteen blows more than were necessary to kill her.

On returning from mass that morning in the company of his farm-hand John Feehan, Daniel found her slumped in the kitchen in a pool of blood. There was blood spattered on walls, tables, chairs and across the stove. She'd been done to death with a hatchet; it was lying near the body, strands of Margaret's hair still clinging to it. Daniel rushed outside and vomited.

When he'd recovered somewhat he lost no time in alerting his neighbours in the little township of Cullinamore. Somebody got word to the police barracks in town, and within minutes Sergeant Pat O'Rourke and two constables were at the scene. By this time the O'Sullivans' yard was crowded with the curious: angry men wishing to lose no time in apprehending Margaret's killer. Heads were being poked around the door of the kitchen; men had gone inside to comfort the grieving Daniel. Sergeant O'Rourke was having none of it. The crime scene was becoming tainted; vital evidence might be lost.

'I want nothing touched!' he barked. 'Go on home now, lads. If I need your help then I know where to find ye.'

Reluctantly the men departed and the sergeant made a thorough inspection. There was no doubt that the hatchet was the murder weapon. O'Rourke had seen similar injuries before and knew they'd been made using tremendous force. The perpetrator was either a strong man, or one seized by a great frenzy.

'Who could have done it?' he asked Margaret's husband.

But Daniel declared that they hadn't an enemy in the world— with the possible exception of Jeremiah Carey, a young man who'd been making trouble in the parish for many months. He'd fallen out with several farmers who employed him for occasional labour.

With hindsight he should have known, and remembered, another enemy—one who'd had a serious argument with both himself and his dead wife. On more than one occasion this enemy had attacked them, though the harm caused was minor. But no doubt the poor man was still in a state of shock and it would be some time before he could think more clearly.

O'Rourke quizzed him on a possible motive. Daniel couldn't for the life of him think of one. Unless it were theft. The sergeant sought his permission to examine the premises; Daniel and his farm-hand offered to assist him in any way they could.

Sure enough, the house had been ransacked, both upstairs and downstairs. Daniel was missing securities to the value of £500, and £16 16s had been removed from a tin box. There were clothes missing too. What O'Rourke found curious was the fact that the thief had taken only clothes belonging to Margaret. He began to wonder if the murder had been the work of two people: a man and a female accomplice.

He ordered a search of the yard and the surrounding fields. Heavy rain had fallen that Saturday night—indeed it was the heaviest in many weeks—and the yard was still wet and muddy, with plenty of clear footprints. Most of the prints, however, had been made by over-zealous neighbours, therefore it was useless to pursue any clues there.

O'Rourke guessed, though, that the killer—or killers—would not have fled in the direction of the road. At the hour of the murder most of the parishioners were at mass, celebrating Easter, but there was still the chance that someone might spot a stranger furtively leaving the O'Sullivan house. No, had he been in the murderer's shoes, the sergeant would have left by the back door. Sure enough, he found a fresh set of prints to the rear of the house; they led off into a potato field. Only one killer then—or the villains had split up and gone in different directions. To judge from the tracks left in the damp, newly turned earth, the villain who'd taken off through the fields had smallish feet. O'Rourke hoped that the murderer wouldn't change his shoes for a while, for the simple reason that one shoe was clearly bigger than the other. The footprints led away in the general direction of Killorglin.

The men of Cullinamore were convinced, however, that Jeremiah Carey was the perpetrator. He got wind of the manhunt and attempted to flee. But he was cornered and brought to the police barracks in Killorglin. A suspect was needed and Carey fitted the bill—if not the footprints. He was duly charged with the murder of Margaret O'Sullivan. To the satisfaction of all (and the stupefaction of O'Rourke) he confessed. He'd come to the farmhouse when the woman was alone, he said, and demanded money. When she refused to give him any he'd split her head with a hatchet and made off with £29.

The difficulty for Sergeant O'Rourke was that the sum tallied not at all with that quoted by Daniel O'Sullivan. The farmer had been very specific about it: £16 16s was missing. Moreover there was no mention of the *real* haul, the £500 in shares: Daniel and Margaret's life-savings. O'Rourke decided to release Carey and withdraw the charges against him. He was going to talk to the people of Cullinamore and beyond—to the entire population of Killorglin if needs be. It was a particularly vicious murder, and one that appeared to have no military significance. His superiors were clamouring for an arrest; if obedience to civil law were seen to be falling apart in County Kerry then what hope was there for the country?

As his inquiries progressed on the Monday following the killing, the sergeant cursed the fact that the perpetrator had chosen Easter Sunday above all days to commit the crime. Just about everybody had been at mass at the time, and the few who hadn't attended mass had remained indoors, as had Margaret O'Sullivan.

But there had been two exceptions: the brothers William and Timothy O'Neill, farming boys who lived about a mile outside Killorglin, on the road to the O'Sullivan house. At about eleven in the morning, when the roads were deserted, they'd met a woman approaching hurriedly from the direction of Cullinamore. She was dressed in a shawl that looked to the lads as though it didn't belong to her; it didn't match her shabby skirt and torn stockings. The youths couldn't help but notice that she was concealing something under the shawl and that her whole demeanour was suspect. She'd had fresh mud on her boots—a great deal of it. Her name was Hannah Flynn.

————

There were many Hannah Flynns in rural Ireland in post-Edwardian times. In a era when social benefits were non-existent and not every family could afford to keep their children at school, girls like Hannah were disadvantaged. She grew up and came of age without 'prospects', and there was nothing else for it but to go into domestic service. She was not the brightest light on the

Christmas tree—indeed, most people in the parish thought of her as extremely feeble minded. She could neither read nor write her own name, couldn't rightly say if she were twenty-nine or thirty.

Her eldest brother had inherited the family farm, the rest of her siblings had left the area, and Hannah lived alone in a miserable cabin about a mile west of Killorglin. The money she earned as a servant was barely enough to cover her upkeep, with perhaps a little left over for the odd night's entertainment. Her clothes were either hand-me-downs or odd items she scavenged from one source or another.

To Hannah the O'Sullivans were wealthy people. Whether they were good employers is difficult to say. We have it from Daniel O'Sullivan that things were never 'right' between Hannah and his wife. She came to the farm in 1922 and they employed her for a short period. It was soon discovered that she had a habit of stealing small items—she was 'too much of a thief around the place'—and that wouldn't do. Moreover she was wilful and disobedient, and Margaret had 'some unpleasantness' with her. She had to go.

But Hannah had not gone quietly. At the time of her sacking she swore to Daniel that she'd 'have your life', a threat he'd dismissed as the ravings of a bitter woman. Evidently, though, Hannah was more aggrieved than the couple had imagined because for a long time afterwards she'd come to their yard after nightfall, roaring obscenities and hurling stones at the house.

Nor was she averse to physical violence. She was a big woman and the other servant, John Feehan, had a healthy respect for her strength. Not long after her dismissal he was carting a load of turf to the O'Sullivan home when Hannah sprang into the road. She 'commandeered' the cart, claiming it in lieu of wages she said were owing to her.

And there the annoyance ended—or so it seemed to the O'Sullivans. Neither could have known or understood the fury that was building up in Hannah's poor demented and deluded mind.

Again Sergeant O'Rourke went over the statement made to him

by the two young brothers who'd met Hannah on the road that Easter Sunday. He knew her, though not well. He knew that she was strong enough to have dealt the hatchet blows that had caused such frightful mutilation. There was, however, even more compelling evidence: the woman was wearing two odd shoes: one longer and broader than the other. They matched exactly those that had made the footprints in the potato field behind the O'Sullivan farmhouse. And if any doubt remained, there was the matter of the shawl she was wearing. It fitted the description of the one missing from the dead woman's house. To Sergeant O'Rourke it looked as much out of keeping with the rest of Hannah's clothing as a regimental horsecloth on a donkey.

When Hannah was arrested and brought in for questioning she swore she'd travelled to Tralee on the Saturday evening. She'd gone there with the promise of work, she said, and hadn't returned to the parish until about 2 pm on Sunday. This was feasible. Tralee is about eighteen miles away, within walking distance. Hannah declared that when she got there she found out that the wages offered were too low. She'd stayed overnight 'in a house in the town' and set out the following morning at seven.

But O'Rourke knew she couldn't have been in Tralee that night because a reliable witness reported seeing her in the Cullinamore area at 10 pm. She'd been walking in the direction of the O'Sullivan home.

Had the murderous intent been there that Saturday night? Had Hannah decided to reignite her old feud with the O'Sullivans? Or had she looked in through a window, seen three people in the house—Daniel, Margaret and John Feehan—and decided to return when Margaret was alone? We cannot ever know because Hannah told the police none of these things.

When she went on trial for murder on 27 February 1924 she likewise remained silent on her movements and motivation. The court at the Dublin Commission accepted without hesitation the defence's plea that Hannah was too feeble-minded to be accountable for her actions. She made a pathetic figure in the dock, facing Mr Justice Pimm. He could barely understand her and had to repeatedly call on her counsel to 'translate' her answers for him. At one point Pimm turned to the jury and told them that he'd support any recommendation to mercy.

Nevertheless the assembled jurors, legal men and members of the public were given a lurid account of Margaret O'Sullivan's injuries. Though there were many in the courtroom who'd become inured to extreme violence throughout the civil war, few had been present at the trial of a 'civilian' capable of inflicting such injuries. Most were horrified, and dismayed that this accused woman appeared to show no remorse at all. Sane or insane, Hannah had done a monstrous deed, had slain an innocent woman whose only 'crime' was to scold her on occasion and dismiss her for pilfering.

Justice Pimm sent the jury away, but they returned within a half hour unable to reach a verdict. They went away a second time and returned within the hour. Hannah was guilty of murder.

The jury recommended clemency, in light of the accused's mental state. It is an odd thing that the judge did not accept this plea—even though he himself had suggested mercy in the first place. Something he'd heard or seen in the course of the trial had caused him to change his mind.

Had he caught Hannah's eye and seen something irredeemably wicked there? Had he misinterpreted a look, a gesture, a turn of phrase? If so, the court transcripts do not record it. He donned the black cap and sentenced Hannah to death, to be hanged on St Patrick's Day, 17 March 1924.

She broke down and had to be assisted from the court. Sentence was duly carried out and her body interred within the walls of Mountjoy Gaol, Dublin.

BRIDIE WALSH AND THE LETHAL LEMONADE

U p above the west Cork village of Meelin, standing proud of the granite slopes of Knockacummer mountain, lies Moylan's Rock. The village and the rock are related by folklore. When Celtic deities ruled this remote part of Ireland the goddess Moylan found herself betrothed against her will to a man she didn't love. Defying her family, she fled to the Newmarket area and was given sanctuary by the local people.

But gods are gods and have ways of knowing things; it wasn't long before her father learned of her whereabouts. He dispatched his men to fetch his errant daughter. Moylan got wind of their approach, summoned her magic powers and took to the air. She alighted on a rock above the village, from whence she made her escape through the ether, reaching safety (some say) at the Blessed Well in Ballinatona. From that time on, the village was named in her honour, as was the rock that had assisted her desperate flight.

By a strange irony the village of Meelin once harboured another woman who sought escape from a loveless marriage, and Ballinatona was to be the place where her husband drew his last, agonizing breath. Her name was Bridie Connell, and hers is as tragic a story as any that has come down to us from Celtic mythology.

She was born in 1898 to a poor but respectable Cork family. Her 'chances' were not good; she had little to offer by way of financial dowry, and so it was that her family considered her fortunate when a casual farm labourer named Michael Walsh proposed marriage. Bridie accepted at once and the match was sanctified in the parish church of Meelin in August 1919. Walsh was forty-four; the bride was nineteen. No eyebrows were raised. Such differences in age were considered by the country folk to be as routine as yoking a horse to a plough. Scandalized eyes would, however, have been on the belly that the newly named Bridie Walsh was doing her best to conceal: she was six months pregnant with the bridegroom's child.

We can only guess at Bridie's feelings as she walked down the aisle on her husband's arm. She might actually have loved him—or imagined she did. What is as good as certain, though, is that Michael Walsh had no love—or indeed any kind of affection—for her. He'd already asserted his conjugal rights months before marriage and would go on to show his utter disdain and disregard for her.

Bridie heard the warning bells sounding when the marriage was not even a week old. Michael simply left her—without so much as a by-your-leave, without a care for how she was going to cope. He packed his bag and left her alone, with a baby on the way.

To be sure, she'd known of his work situation. He'd told her that his employment was a fickle affair. Nothing was certain: he was at the beck and call of those who had need of his services. He had to go where the work was. Bridie had understood this. What Michael had not told her—but what people had whispered to her during the courtship—was that he was an alcoholic and a man devoid of all sense of responsibility. A man, it seems, who'd never grown up.

Bridie did indeed hear the alarm bells on Michael's first desertion. She ignored them, hoping that he'd return in a day or two; in a week, in a month. But he stayed away all that autumn. Nor was he there when Bridie gave birth to their first child. She was penniless and had to borrow money from her family, who grudgingly gave her barely enough to feed herself and the baby throughout that long winter.

Spring came and there was still no sign of Michael Walsh. He could have met with an accident somewhere, and died, for all Bridie knew. There was no letter, no postcard, no word passed from friend to friend. She didn't know if he was even in the country.

And then, as unexpectedly as he'd left the previous August, he showed up at the door of their cottage. There was no money. That had all gone on drink.

In reply to Bridie's natural question as to where he'd been the past ten months, Michael told her only that he'd been 'working'. Evidently he felt under no obligation to offer her a better explanation. She meant nothing to him; his baby child even less. Bridie represented no more than a place where he could pass a few days, a bed where he could enjoy gratis sex, and be on his way whenever he felt like it.

And that is precisely what he did. He remained with her for three weeks, then was off again, leaving his wife pregnant for the second time.

Two years went by, during which time Bridie suffered incredible hardship. Her first child died soon after the birth of her second, and Michael Walsh neither knew nor cared.

On his return from his second spell of 'working', Bridie told him that enough was enough. This wasn't how she expected married life to be. But her remonstrations only had the effect of driving her feckless husband away yet again—this time the following day.

It was 1922. All told, the pair had lived together as a married couple for a little over a month. Seven more years were to pass before Bridie saw her husband again. By that time her situation had changed dramatically. And, during those seven years of solitude in the remote bogland above the village of Meelin, something terrible had been taking form in the deserted woman's mind. Michael Walsh might have broken her heart but he hadn't crushed her spirit. She was determined that he was going to pay for his sins.

By 1929, ten years after her wedding, Bridie had given up carrying a torch for her shiftless husband. That she waited so long is less a reflection on her gullibility as on the predicament of a married woman in pre-war rural Ireland. Her rights were severely limited; in the eyes of Church and State (de Valera had succeeded in bonding the two institutions as never before) the married woman was no more than a chattel of her husband. Divorce was utterly out of the question. All property was in the husband's name. An abused woman could only fall back on her family and friends; she'd get no real help anywhere else.

That Michael Walsh had abused his wife and his marriage was never in doubt. Although the abuse was not physical it was just as vicious—if not more so. He'd displayed a heartlessness that was unforgivable. Moreover, rumours would reach Bridie's ears from time to time. Rumours about Michael's womanizing up and down the county. She'd married a wastrel, a drinker and a lecher.

She didn't deserve this. Bridie was a well brought-up woman who liked to think of herself as one of nature's poets. As a girl she'd had romantic visions of the married idyll, thinking about how one man would, as her favourite poet Yeats put it, love the 'pilgrim soul' within her. As the marriage matured and children came and grew, that same man would love the sorrows of her 'changing face'.

She wrote poems herself: simple verses and love songs. They showed the girlish musings of an intelligent and passionate woman. In other circumstances Bridie Connell would have in some sense made her mark on the world. Marriage to Michael Walsh had robbed her of her dreams.

But at some point she decided to cut her losses and move on, to try and start all over again. She brought her surviving child to her mother in Meelin who, with great reluctance, agreed to take care of the girl until Bridie 'found her feet again'. Now thirty, she went in search of work, finding it quickly as a domestic servant in the home of David Walsh of Kilmallock, County Limerick. She reverted to her maiden name, put her wedding band aside, and to all intents and purposes Bridie Connell was a single woman 'doing for' the Walshes of Kilmallock.

We don't know if Bridie encouraged male attention. It seems unlikely, given her unfortunate experience of the opposite sex. Nor was she a particularly good-looking woman. Nevertheless she met, at a social, a garrulous and friendly farm labourer named Bill Frawley. A native of Limerick, he was thirty-five, and seemed to Bridie to be everything that her absentee husband was not. Frawley told her he loved her, and Bridie was convinced he was sincere. They talked of marriage.

There was, of course, a rather large and irritating fly in the ointment, and it answered to the name of Michael Walsh.

Now it is a fact that family law then—as now—made provision for the circumstances Bridie found herself in. Were a man to go missing for seven years then his wife could reasonably presume him dead. This ruling has always been particularly useful in the case of deepwater fishermen, who might be lost at sea without their bodies ever being recovered. Michael Walsh hadn't been seen or heard from in seven years. Bridie would therefore have been well within her rights to have him legally declared dead, leaving her free to marry again if she so chose.

She did no such thing. To be fair—in light of what was to come—a woman in Bridie's situation was unlikely to be familiar with the finer points of family law. Nor would Bill Frawley have been any the wiser: he could neither read nor write. In any event it's improbable that she told him of Michael's existence. Such an admission would certainly have jeopardized her prospects of remarrying.

There is every reason to assume that Bridie knew perfectly well that Michael Walsh was alive and well. Country people talk, and they talk in particular about their old neighbours and kinsmen. Even if Michael had ventured farther than an adjoining county, word of his activities would have trickled back to Meelin and its environs. He still had family there; understandably Bridie had little truck with them, with the exception of Jeremiah Walsh, a kindly man, quite unlike his brother Michael.

There was also Tim Walsh, another brother, and one whom

Bridie would visit with great reluctance, and only on the off-chance of receiving news of her wayward spouse. If anybody knew what became of Michael then it was Tim, who liked his pint and glass as much as Michael did and drank a naggin or two with him whenever occasion allowed.

Bridie had a plan. Whether it was fully formed in her head at the time is impossible to say. It does seem that she did her best at first to seek a reconciliation with Michael; she might have wished to give him one last chance. She was a devout Catholic after all, and believed in her heart that her dalliance with Frawley was immoral. Michael Walsh might treat the sacrament of matrimony with contempt: his wife did not.

Her work with the Walshes in Limerick had enabled her to put some money by, and she used this to travel back to County Cork and set up a home for herself in the town of Newmarket. It was November 1930.

That Christmas she went to the local offices of what was then the *Cork Examiner* and took out a series of four classified advertisements. In the Personal column she inserted the following.

If Michael Walsh, formerly of Meelin, will communicate with Heffernan & Co., Kanturk, he will hear something to his advantage.

The lure was irresistible, implying as it did that there was money in the offing, perhaps an inheritance, at any rate a windfall of some kind.

Michael took the bait. Where he'd been, Bridie was not to learn. He'd been 'working' as usual. He duly replied to the box number contained in the final small notice, that of 3 January 1931. We do not know how disappointed he must have been to learn that there was no windfall as expected. But he was on his uppers as always, having spent what little he'd earned on drink. He was glad that the woman who'd shown such forbearance in the past seemed prepared to put up with him yet again.

This time he remained with Bridie for four whole months—the

longest stretch they'd had together since their wedding day. At first they stayed at Jones's Hotel in Kanturk. Later they found temporary accommodation with the Callaghan family in the village of Clash, close to Kanturk, where Michael was employed as a farmhand. Bridie could finally take their ten-year-old daughter off her mother's hands.

But she might as well have tried to tame a March hare as persuade Michael to mend his footloose ways. Her good-for-nothing spouse didn't relish the thought of providing for a wife and child. They argued about it, Bridie reminding him of his marriage vows. His response was brutal. He was folding his tents again, he told her, and moving to the farm of Jeremiah Brown. Alone. What, she asked, would she do in that case? She could hardly stay on at the Callaghans' if he didn't work for them any longer. Michael shrugged. It was none of his affair. His wife and child could travel the roads for all he cared.

'You're a fine strong woman,' he said. 'You're well able to go into service to support yourself.' He jerked a thumb in the direction of the yard. 'You can take the cart, and the donkey. Now, be gone with you.'

Devastated and bitter, Bridie left with her daughter for Newmarket. It was 26 April. Michael Walsh would be dead within a fortnight.

———

The narrative grows a little confused at this point. We have to sift and weigh the testimony of a number of witnesses, testimony that largely agrees on the principal events, yet in the details—where the devil by tradition lies—is conflicting.

We know for instance that Michael Walsh moved within days from the Callaghan farm and the accommodation he'd shared with Bridie and their daughter. On 29 April he moved into digs in Ballinatona, near to the Blessed Well where once the goddess Moylan found refuge. Michael found *his* accommodation with Jeremiah Brown, his wife and their two sons. The Browns were farmers and needed his help with the spring planting. For one thing could be said about Michael Walsh: drunkard and irresponsible husband though he was, he never shirked work and was regarded as being a good hand to have around the place.

On 6 May Farmer Brown, his family and the new farmhand had eaten their evening meal and were sitting at the fire when at about 7.30 a knock sounded. Joseph Brown, the younger son, opened the door. Standing there in the gathering twilight was Bridie Connell. She spotted Michael.

'I want you,' she said simply.

He was sober and his mind was clear. He suspected that his wife had come demanding money. He may have suspected that Bridie wanted to embarrass him in front of the Browns. In any event he didn't wish to make a scene, and neither presumably did Bridie. Michael excused himself and went to meet her.

'He wasn't surprised to see me,' Bridie would say later.

The two set off together in the direction of the village. By now night had fallen.

Bridie asked her husband what he intended to do.

'I'll not settle, Bridie,' he said, 'until I've earned enough to buy a house for us.'

'And until then? How am I supposed to live? Isn't Jeremiah Brown only after paying you a week's wages.'

'Well, I've spent it.'

'On drink, I suppose.'

'Well, if I did, what of it? I earned it and I spent it.'

Bridie proceeded to read him the riot act. He gave in.

'Meet me on Sunday in Newmarket,' he said. 'I'll have my wages then. When I have it, it's yours. It won't be much but it's the best I can do.'

Bridie rounded on him.

'What about the child?' she demanded. 'Who's going to provide for her? Must she and I go begging through the country and everything?'

The row started in earnest. It's surprising that nobody heard them arguing because they went at it hammer and tongs for an hour at least. Bridie laid into him, complaining about his drinking and his fecklessness, criticizing him for choosing to work for the Browns rather than the Callaghans where his wife and daughter were. No, he said, he'd rather hang himself than stay there. Would he, she asked, support her now at least? Would she stop nagging him? Neither would give in to the other.

It was the quarrelling that gave them both a dry throat. We don't know for sure who suggested that they could quench their thirst with a bottle of lemonade. It would be too easy to say that Bridie alone could have made this decision, that Michael—given his overfondness for alcohol—would naturally have chosen porter. But we are in 1931, a time when only slatterns and 'loose women' frequented Irish public houses. Michael wouldn't have dreamed of inviting his wife to join him in a glass of beer.

In the event it was Bridie who called round to the rear of Quinlan's in Meelin. Her knock was answered by Bridget Conway, the publican wife. She was used to such back-door sales; a furtive purchase of a bottle of stout or spirits was customary among the more 'private' individuals in the village. It was 9.15 pm.

According to Mrs Conway, Bridie paid for the bottle of lemonade and accepted a glass 'to bring over to my husband'. She poured the drink, handed back the empty bottle, and drank off about three-quarters of the glass. Then she bade the pub owner goodnight and went off into the shadows where Michael Walsh awaited her. Within minutes she was back with the empty glass.

Bridie would insist later that they continued on their way for a while, the argument being laid to rest for the time being. Michael lit a pipe, wished her Godspeed and reminded her of their appointment in Newcastle that coming Sunday. They parted amicably, Bridie returning to her temporary lodgings and her child; her sister Mary and husband John Brosnan had kindly given them a roof over their heads.

The night was clear with an almost full moon to guide the wayfarer. At about 11.00 a man whose farm adjoined that of Jeremiah Brown's heard somebody out in the lane roaring with pain. On going to investigate he found Michael Walsh doubled up in agony and retching uncontrollably. The farmer helped Michael as far as the Browns' yard and summoned the family from their beds.

Brown and his sons were dismayed at Michael's condition. They brought him inside. There was, according to Jeremiah, 'a terrible sweat on his face and he had one hand on his back'. Joseph hurried for the doctor.

Strychnine ranks among the deadliest poisons known to science. To administer strychnine to a human being is one of the most appalling and unforgivable methods of murder. The victim dies by convulsing himself to death. We're told that when in the throes of a strychnine-induced spasm the victim feels as if he's about to break his spine, or in any case that he's about to effect great internal damage on himself.

Dr Arthur Verling, Dispensary Medical Officer of Newmarket and GP for Meelin, came at the run, he being almost certain— from what Joseph Brown breathlessly told him—that Michael Walsh had ingested some of the lethal poison. He knew that there was perhaps too much of it lying about in pantries and cupboards up and down the land. Farmers used it to keep the rat population down, but strychnine had a nasty habit of finding its way into animal feed, felling sheepdogs and livestock on occasion. It was also known to lay low a human being or two if one wasn't careful.

He found Michael Walsh in a pitiful state. It was a little after midnight and the unfortunate man had been borne to his bed: a rough mattress on the floor of an upstairs room. Jeremiah junior was away to fetch Father Breen, the parish priest. Verling was convinced right away that the good father's ministrations would be more effective than his own: Michael Walsh was ready to enter the hereafter.

His body was convulsing at the rate of about four spasms per minute. He was still conscious but seemed scarcely aware of his surroundings. His eyes were wild and staring into oblivion. Dr Verling read the fear of God there.

The doctor administered chloroform and twice flushed Michael's stomach and intestines. It was as he'd suspected: strychnine poisoning. In his opinion the victim's 'goose was cooked if something could not be done for him quickly'.

The priest arrived and gave Michael the last rites. But there was no ambulance, despite Dr Verling's repeated attempts to summon one. Eventually, at about 4.20 am, one did arrive. It was too late. Michael Walsh died on his way to Kanturk hospital.

Nobody involved got any sleep that night. A tragedy of such proportions was relatively unknown in the sleepy little village of Meelin. As dawn broke, the news had already travelled far and wide. Who, the people asked themselves, could have done such a thing?

For there was no doubt in anybody's mind that Michael hadn't poisoned himself. Drunkard though he was, and given to moodiness, he was still an unlikely candidate for suicide. And why choose strychnine as the method of self-destruction? Madness. One wouldn't do it.

He might, it was argued, have swallowed the poison inadvertently. Again, it was unlikely. Strychnine is extremely bitter. In order to disguise its acridity one would have to mix in honey or sugar or treacle.

Or perhaps lemonade.

In the town of Newmarket the rumours got underway and tongues began to wag. It wasn't long before the finger of guilt was pointing at Bridie. All who knew her were aware of Michael's past, and if anybody in the parish had motive then it was his abused wife.

The authorities shared this view. First, however, it had to be established for certain how the victim died. Sure enough, a post-mortem examination revealed the presence of strychnine in Michael's body. It was a small amount but it was enough to kill a man. Had Dr Verling not irrigated his stomach Michael would have died much, much sooner. Somebody had fed him a truly massive dose.

As luck would have it, Mrs Conway the pub owner hadn't yet got round to washing the glass that had contained the lemonade. The Gardaí examined it and found traces of the poison. A suspicion had become a near certainty. They went to Bridie's sister's house and spoke to the suspect. Bridie denied all knowledge. Even when they found crystals of strychnine in a pocket of her coat she continued to protest her innocence. They had no choice but to arrest her, on 11 June 1931.

———

Following on from a preliminary hearing in Kanturk, the case proper came to trial on Monday, 15 June, in the Central Criminal Court, Dublin. It was to last for two days.

Bridie was clever—or at any rate cleverer than the average poisoner. She hadn't done anything as obvious as procure the poison in Meelin or the vicinity. Nor had she bought it immediately prior to administering it. No, she'd planned the deed many weeks earlier, and in another place—so argued the State prosecutor.

It began, it seems, on or towards the end of April, when Bridie and Michael were still living in the Callaghan house. The rats, he told her, were 'having the run of the place' and would she mind going and buying some poison.

'Get it yourself!' she responded. They'd had words as usual that morning and she was in no mood for running errands for a man she despised.

But evidently Michael's request had set her thinking, and when they parted company some days later—she being unceremoniously shown the road—the notion of poison must have been fresh in her mind.

She moved into her sister's house but was equally determined not to spend too much time under another woman's roof. She'd found work before in County Limerick and was sure she could find it again. In the event, she was disappointed. No doubt this was a very bitter blow—and she knew at whose door she could lay the blame.

We know that on the afternoon of 6 May, the day of the murder, Bridie went to the village of Kilmallock, Limerick, the place where she'd worked for two years. However, James Horgan, the local pharmacist, didn't know her, she never having been in his shop before. She handed over a note that had apparently been written by David Walsh, Bridie's old employer. It requested the chemist to sell to the bearer, 'Bridget Murphy', a quantity of poison needed to put down for some dogs that had been making a nuisance of themselves.

In reality Bridie had written the note herself, as a handwriting analyst would testify. She'd also signed the poison register. It read: 'David Walsh, per Bridget Murphy'. Horgan assumed that her employer required strychnine. He filled a small bottle with a quantity of the poison, corked it tightly, wrapped it in paper and handed it over.

Killmallock is close to the Cork-Limerick border and a little over twenty miles from Meelin. In her donkey and cart—the parting 'gift' from her husband—Bridie would have made the return journey long before nightfall. And so it was that she presented herself that evening at the Browns' farm, poison in pocket and ready to confront the man who'd given her so much grief.

She testified at her trial that she'd handed the bottle of poison to her husband. Had he not asked her to buy it for him? Her defending counsellor tried to make a case of suicide. Walsh, he submitted, intended taking his own life, then returning the poisoned lemonade to Bridie. He wanted to take her with him when he departed this life.

But it wouldn't wash, as anybody in that Dublin courtroom could clearly see. Fact: Mr Horgan the pharmacist swore that he'd corked the bottle very securely and put his stamp on it. How then to account for the grains of strychnine—one of a half gram, the other of one tenth of a gram—that the Gardaí had found in Bridie's coat pocket?

And Mrs Conway swore under oath that she'd seen Bridie drink three-quarters of the lemonade. The sequence was wrong.

The jury of twelve men, however, gave Bridie the benefit of the doubt, acquitting her of all charges. But the people of Meelin remained unconvinced. No one but Bridie Connell had a better reason for wanting Michael Walsh out of the way. No one else had either motive or opportunity of administering the poison. No one else stood to benefit from his death.

One would like to believe that those twelve men believed in their hearts that Bridie was guilty, but felt compassion for this woman who'd suffered so much by marrying the wrong man. Had they found her guilty of murder—and murder it had to be, rather than the lesser charge of manslaughter—then Justice Hanna, the presiding judge, would have had to sentence her to hanging. Or commute the death sentence to life imprisonment. In 1931 'life' meant life behind bars. It would be heartening to believe that those jurors chose to spare Bridie one or the other punishment.

CHARLOTTE BRYANT AND THE RAGGLE-TAGGLE GYPSY

'*I do love you, Tess—O, I do—it is all come back!' he said, tightening his arms round her with fervid pressure. 'But how do you mean—you have killed him?'*

'I mean that I have,' she murmured in a reverie.

What, bodily? Is he dead?'

'Yes. He heard me crying about you, and he bitterly taunted me; and called you by a foul name; and then I did it. My heart could not bear it. He had nagged me about you before. And then I dressed myself and came away to find you.'

Thomas Hardy, TESS OF THE D'URBERVILLES

The Duke of Wellington called them 'camp followers' and reckoned they had a bad influence on his soldiers. They were the prostitutes and good-time girls who pleasured the men when they were far from their loved ones. They were associated with permanent camps too, in towns and cities that required a garrison, whether for the people's protection or to keep those same people subdued.

It was 1922. Frederick John Bryant was serving as a military policeman with his regiment, the Dorsets, in the walled city of

Londonderry. Seventy-six years would pass before its official name was changed to Derry City, but at the time of writing those with vested interests in retaining the 'London' prefix stick doggedly to its use. For it is a fact that the 'Maiden City' has long been a contentious place. In Fred Bryant's soldiering days it was the north-westernmost outpost of the British Empire in these islands, close enough to the new border with the Free State to be a target for republicans, hence the size and might of the garrison.

Bryant and his fellow servicemen fraternized at their peril with the local population of this predominantly Catholic city—with the ordinary women in particular. And so it was that Derry's ladies of easy virtue did good trade with the sex-starved young soldiers. Among the ladies was Charlotte McHugh, a beautiful nineteen-year-old. She could neither read nor write but she could weave a spell of talk around any man. And she loved to have men about her. Though not a prostitute in the strict sense she was known throughout the army barracks for the generous dispensation of her amorous favours.

Fred Bryant fell in love with her, and was determined that he alone should have her, rather than share her affections with others. What he didn't know, however, was that Charlotte McHugh saw in him a way out of a life that was far from comfortable. Her family strongly disapproved of her 'consorting' with His Majesty's forces, as did her friends. She was shunned by neighbours, and more than once she heard through the grapevine that her liaisons with soldiers might get her into trouble. Girls who slept with soldiers were sometimes tarred and feathered. Charlotte had a plan, a means of escaping all this: she told Bryant that she was pregnant with his child.

She knew that his tour of duty was approaching its end. Moreover, he'd told her on many occasions that he wanted to quit the army. He'd had enough of bad pay and bad rations. He wished to return to his native Dorsetshire and do what he did best: work on the land. For Charlotte, the idyll of England that Bryant painted was an alluring one. Anything was better than grubby Derry with its shirt factories and industry-induced squalor. To be sure, she'd dreamed of being whisked away to glamorous London by a wealthy Englishman, but Dorset would do for a start. She'd see what would come of it when she got there. . . .

So Fred Bryant was a father-to-be. He was twenty-six and the idea of fatherhood appealed to him. He saw himself living the good life with the raven-haired Ulster beauty, being the envy of all his old friends. They duly left Derry, Bryant obtained his discharge and they married in the cathedral city of Wells in Somerset.

If the young man had harboured any doubts about his bride then they didn't at once manifest themselves. He could hardly fail to notice, however, that Charlotte's pregnancy lasted an uncommonly long time—they'd been married well over a year before the child was actually born. He'd been duped.

But events had overtaken the birth of Ernest, the Bryants' first child. Fred had no trouble finding work on his beloved land. England was still smarting from the devastation caused by the Great War. A whole generation had been wiped out in the trenches; there was an acute shortage of young men needed to work the farms. Fred secured a promising job as a farmhand near the village of Over Compton, close to the town of Yeovil. The position came complete with a 'tied' cottage—as long as he remained working for the farmer then the couple could call the house their own. Fred Bryant was a happy man.

The years passed. His wife bore three more children. She was growing steadily restless though. Thomas Hardy might have sung the praises of this, the county of his birth and the setting for most of his West Country tales, but to somebody like Charlotte, who'd grown up in the bustle and excitement of the big city, Dorset had proved to be a let-down. She'd long resigned herself to the fact that London was a dream that could never become reality. But as time went by she was beginning to remember her native city with fondness. She was coming to the realization that even Derry, for all its faults, was preferable to the tedium of the countryside. She saw no one from one end of the week to the other. There were no soldiers with full pay-packets to carouse with, no more drunken fumbles in alleyways. Charlotte was bored with married life.

Yeovil, however, was no more than a short haywain ride away, and Charlotte availed of every opportunity to travel there—without her husband. While Fred Bryant was at work or minding the four children, his wife was living it up in the pubs of the town, resuming her life as a strumpet. It wasn't long before she was acquiring a reputation in the district. The men even had nicknames for her: 'Killarney Kate' and 'Black Bess'.

We might wonder why Fred put up with Charlotte's profligacy. The truth was that he—soldier though he'd been—was more than a little afraid of her. She had a wicked temper, especially when drunk. She could fly off the handle at the smallest provocation and browbeat her husband with her sharp tongue. He should have read the signs when they were courting in Derry—heaven knows they were clear enough. But his infatuation with the Irish beauty had overruled his common sense.

Nor was Fred's employer too pleased with Charlotte Bryant. The farmer appreciated her husband's hard work, but he was a practising and God-fearing Christian as well. He didn't take kindly to the idea of one of his cottages being occupied by a prostitute—for that was what Charlotte had become. For years now she'd been charging good money for her 'services', a lot more than what Fred was earning. Much of her income went on fine clothes, scent, and other luxuries that were foreign to the wife of a humble farm worker.

It seems, however, that Fred Bryant didn't wholly disapprove of his wife's whoring. He was also profiting from her immoral earnings.

'I don't care what she does,' he confided to a neighbour. 'Four pounds a week is better than thirty shillings.'

By 1933 this last sum was Fred's weekly wage. His wife was bringing in three times his wages and he wasn't complaining.

Not even when a man named Parsons showed up at the cottage and asked for lodgings.

———

Leonard Edward Parsons was a member of what we nowadays refer to as the travelling community. In December 1933, when he caught Charlotte's eye, he was known variably as a 'gypsy', a 'horse-trader'—or a 'thieving scoundrel', depending on whether he'd crossed you or not. They met in Yeovil when Parsons' business activities brought him to the town.

He had a home of his own, and a family too. Priscilla Loveridge was his common-law wife, by whom he had four children. They lived in Devon and Leonard divided his time between them and his new love-interest, Charlotte.

It's hard to know what to make of the relationship that emerged between the Bryants and the lodger. It appears that Fred and Leonard got on very well, often drinking together at the village inn. At the same time the gypsy was openly cuckolding Fred, and Fred seemed not to mind too much. Was he so under the thumb of his overbearing wife that he was prepared to indulge her, to the point where she was having sex with another man in Fred's own home? Or was he afraid of losing her? It does seem that he genuinely loved her.

Whatever the real reason, Fred's boss was sick of it. It was bad enough that Charlotte was prostituting herself with half the men in the neighbourhood. Now she was bringing her sins home with her. He sacked Fred—which automatically meant eviction for all of them: the Bryants, their children and the gypsy.

But Fred quickly found another position near Sherborne, in a place called Coombe. The deal was the same: a job with a cottage tied to it. The Bryants' domestic arrangements were likewise resumed as if nothing had happened. Once more Parsons moved in with them.

Charlotte's infatuation with the gypsy was growing, becoming more serious with each passing month. She wanted to spend all her time with him. Often Fred had to sleep on the sofa while Leonard shared the marital bed with his wife.

It must have been around this time—in late 1934—when the idea of murder entered Charlotte's head. Understandably, Fred was getting fed up with the situation, threatening in his mild-mannered way to show Leonard the door. But the Derrywoman had no intention of losing the man she was besotted with.

'Would you marry me,' she asked the gypsy over and over, 'if I were a widow?'

The answer, though Leonard did not speak it aloud, was 'no'. He was not in love with Charlotte and never had been. To him she was no more than an extended roll in the hay, somebody who enjoyed a night of passion as much as he did. One 'wife' and a clatter of children were enough for him 'to be getting on with'. Nor do we know how many other women he was seeing. He moved about the West Country a good deal, going where the livestock fairs were held. Sometimes Charlotte would travel with him, claiming to be his wife. One of their jaunts took them as far as Plymouth, and she availed of the opportunity to look in on a sister she had living there, whom she hadn't seen in some time.

Mostly, though, Leonard travelled alone to the various fairs. The traditional horse-fair was—and still is—a social occasion. When the wheeling and dealing was done, men like Leonard would congregate in the inns to drink some of their profits, and women like Charlotte would be on hand to help them to do so.

As the year approached its end, however, the horse-trading slackened off. Though Leonard's infatuation for Charlotte was on the wane he was nevertheless spending more and more time with the Bryants. It was at this point that Fred Bryant decided that enough was enough for him as well. He ordered Leonard out. There was a terrible scene. When the gypsy left, Charlotte went with him.

The pair rented rooms in the town of Dorchester, a little way from the coast and twenty miles due south of Sherbourne. In order to reach it the traveller has to pass through Cerne Abbas, and Charlotte insisted they call a halt there. She had Leonard make a small detour with the cart so that she might pause and admire the famous Cerne Giant, of which she'd heard so much. Sure enough, the huge figure, cut into the chalk hill by unknown hands, was a source of awe for Charlotte. She stood for a long time gazing up at it. Then she made a coarse joke, referring to the size and enduring quality of the figure's most prominent feature:

its erect penis. We don't know if Leonard was amused.

They didn't remain long in Dorchester. Charlotte missed her children. She returned alone to Coombe and was welcomed back by her long-suffering husband. A few days later they met Leonard Parsons in an inn in Sherborne, somehow came to an amicable arrangement, and the horse-trader was allowed back into the Bryant home.

She'd got her way again but still Charlotte wasn't satisfied. She wanted it all: her lover and her children. Fred had become a liability. He would have to go.

————

The first attack came in May 1935. Fred ate lunch, cooked as usual by Charlotte, and went off to work in the fields. Before long he complained to his workmates of a severe stomach upset. He was taken short and forced to run for the bushes to relieve his diarrhoea. His workmates laughed at first but very soon realized the seriousness of the attack. Fred was vomiting, had a burning pain in his mouth and gullet. The pain and vomiting grew worse. It was decided it was best to bring the stricken man home and to fetch the doctor.

Oddly enough the doctor's first diagnosis was poisoning by arsenic. He'd seen it often enough in his practice. The poison, when taken in small doses, can induce great pain and discomfort while not being life threatening. Caught early, its symptoms can be treated easily.

But arsenic has the disquieting characteristic of remaining in the body of the victim, accumulating in the tissues, and in the nails and hair. Only over time will it dissipate. If it's administered often but in small doses then it will kill in the end.

The doctor treated Fred and observed that he made a very rapid recovery. So rapid was it that the doctor revised his diagnosis, and decided that Fred's attack was no more serious than gastroenteritis. In a time when hygiene was poor, and the refrigeration of food non-existent, the complaint was a common one. Within a day or two Fred returned to work as if nothing had happened.

Two attacks came in the month of August. Again Fred ate lunch prepared by Charlotte and went to tend the farmer's cattle. Again he took sick, vomiting and experiencing diarrhoea. In fact the symptoms were almost identical to those he'd had two months before. The doctor should, perhaps, have been more cautious but again he diagnosed gastroenteritis, and again Fred recovered quickly—if less quickly than on the first occasion.

It was the second attack of August, though, that gave Fred grounds for suspicion. This time the victim was another man, a fellow farmhand. On that particular day Charlotte had made tea for her husband, and one of the daughters had brought it out to him. Fred wasn't thirsty and had given the tea to a fellow labourer. Almost immediately after drinking it, the man suffered pain and discomfort similar to Fred's, though far less severe.

Fred said nothing to Charlotte, but from that time on he chose to prepare his own meals whenever possible. He made sure that he, not Charlotte, cooked the Sunday dinner; on weekdays they divided the cooking between them. She must have known he suspected her of tampering with his food and drink.

All, however, was not well between Charlotte and her gypsy lover. The passion had cooled. In November Leonard suddenly announced that he was leaving, perhaps never to return. He told a devastated Charlotte that his work was taking him to another part of the county. The real reason was that Leonard had grown tired of their relationship. She might well have loved him but her love was not reciprocated. To her disgust she began to receive word of sightings of the gypsy in the area. He shouldn't have been there at all—he'd given her to understand that he was heading west, in the direction of Somerset.

Charlotte went in search of him. She looked in at all the pubs they used to frequent, hoping that she'd chance upon him sooner or later. But he always seemed to be one step ahead—or so his cronies gave her to understand.

The departure of the horse-trader must have hastened her resolve to do away with her husband. We know this because in November Charlotte befriended a woman who'd just moved into a neighbouring cottage. That in itself was not significant; it would have been considered odd had she not done so, for Lucy Ostler had need of a friend at that time. She was a widow who'd been left to bring up two young children. She could only make ends meet by going into domestic service in Coombe, working not for one household but several. Charlotte offered her some light work around the house.

Later it would be said that Charlotte's show of charity was a cynical ploy, and a cruel attempt to throw suspicion on this unfortunate woman—to have others believe that Lucy Ostler had poisoned Fred. On the face of it, it was a downright stupid piece of reasoning and—given that Charlotte showed great cunning and resource in most areas—a bad lapse in judgement.

In any event Lucy was present in the cottage when the third attack took place. It was 11 December 1935. The symptoms were the same and the wonder is that the GP still did not feel justified in alerting the authorities. Fred once again made a full recovery, though this time it took him a little longer.

Fred Bryant, aged thirty-six and a man in otherwise excellent health, could not have known he was dying. The arsenic lodged in his body had by now accumulated to a frightening degree. It required only one further dose to kill him, and that dose need not be large at all.

———

The final attack came three days before Christmas. It came on a morning when Lucy Ostler was in the Bryant cottage, a fact that seemed more than convenient for Charlotte. Her husband's symptoms were far more severe than before. Having evacuated his bowels he took to his bed, writhing in agony. Lucy looked on, horrified.

'Can you help him?' Charlotte asked. 'I'm no good at nursing.'

And with that she left Fred entirely in the care of the widow. Lucy treated him with her traditional country remedies. She gave him bicarbonate of soda and hot milk. Nothing helped, though, and she urged Charlotte to fetch the doctor.

Fred was rushed to Coldharbour Hospital in Sherborne. He died the following afternoon, on 23 December.

The medical men could no longer ignore the possibility of poison, and alerted the police. The Home Office pathologist was brought in to carry out an autopsy. It revealed the presence in Fred's stomach and other organs of more than four grains of arsenic.

It was a serious case, so serious that the chief constable of the Dorset police chose to enlist the help of London's Metropolitan Police. Chief Detective-Inspector Bell and Detective-Sergeant Tapsell arrived in Sherborne to begin their investigation.

As yet there was no finger pointed at Charlotte, but the men from the CID thought that a search of the Bryant home might throw up some clue to Fred's poisoner. They had Charlotte and her children removed to temporary accommodation at the Public Assistance Institution—the workhouse—in Sturminster Newton, and together with the local constables made a very careful examination of the entire cottage, its yard and outhouses.

First, though, they interviewed those who'd last seen Fred alive, among whom was Lucy Ostler.

Chief Detective-Inspector Bell had never seriously considered her as a prime suspect. For a start she'd had no motive. On the contrary Fred Bryant's death would of necessity be to her disadvantage. She and her children depended on money from the Bryants. Were Fred to die then that little bit of income would dry up; both she and Charlotte would find themselves in the place where Charlotte now sat with her five children: the workhouse.

No, from the start Bell suspected that Lucy was being made a patsy. Fred had had three attacks before she'd even come to live in Coombe; Lucy could have had no hand in any of them. That she was present on the day of the final attack was Charlotte's doing. Had she deliberately made herself scarce and left Lucy to nurse her husband alone? Mrs Ostler had a curious tale to tell.

Following Fred's death and the diagnosis of arsenic poisoning, the Sherborne police had set out for the Bryant home. Charlotte had got wind of their impending visit. She called together her son

Ernest and Lucy, telling them that the place had to be 'cleared up', lest the police think there'd been foul play. She hinted that in such cases the authorities sometimes jumped to the wrong conclusions, attaching undue significance to items that were perfectly innocuous. Items such as tins of weedkiller. . . .

Charlotte went to a cupboard in the living-room and drew out a tin can. It was labelled Eureka, and Lucy recognized it as a popular brand of weedkiller. But Charlotte told her that it contained paraffin for lighting the lamps in the house, a very plausible story in a time when housewives disposed of sturdy tin cans only with reluctance when they could be put to further use.

'I'll get rid of this for a start,' Charlotte said.

Behind the tin, however, was another of the same brand. Lucy opened it and sniffed it. She smelt the unmistakable, strong odour of undiluted weedkiller.

'I must get rid of that too,' Charlotte told her.

It was at that moment that the widow guessed the truth. She was also acutely conscious of the predicament she herself was in.

'Oh, Charlotte,' she said, 'if you've done something to your husband then it'll look very bad for me. I'm the one who nursed him on his deathbed.'

Charlotte dismissed her fears and warned her to keep quiet about the tin of Eureka. She left the cottage with it and returned empty handed some minutes later.

'If nothing is found,' she said to Mrs Ostler, 'then they can't put a rope around my neck.'

She was careless. Bell and Tapsell recovered more than one hundred and fifty suspect items from the Bryant house and surroundings. Of those, no fewer than thirty contained traces of arsenic. To us, at this remove, this might seem like thirty items too many. But it's useful to remember that in 1936 the poison was freely available, although its purchase had to be signed for. Among the items sent to the Home Office forensic laboratory was a tin container that somebody had tried unsuccessfully to incinerate. The label was still legible: it was Eureka weedkiller. Bell knew that Eureka consisted of seventy per cent arsenic.

The fact that somebody had tried to destroy the can of poison seemed to indicate that it had been used to kill Fred Bryant. Bell decided to instigate a search of all the poison registers in the West Country. It was a formidable task and he enlisted the help of every available officer. In the end hundreds of policemen were quizzing chemists in three counties. Somewhere, in some town or other, Bell reasoned, the name Charlotte Bryant would appear on a register.

It was a mistake that would waste many days and tie up much manpower. Until, that is, a local policeman informed his superiors that Charlotte was illiterate and incapable of even writing her own name. This in itself was hardly anything out of the ordinary; in rural England of the 1930s the literacy rate lagged far behind that of modern Britain. But Bell was vexed that no one had thought of it earlier.

As it turned out, Charlotte had been less cautious than Bridie Walsh of County Cork. Whereas the Meelin poisoner had bought her strychnine in the next county, using an assumed name and a forged note, Charlotte had done her deadly shopping closer to home. Not six miles from Coombe, in the town of Yeovil, one of her old haunts, the investigators found a chemist's shop with a very interesting poison register. Somebody—a woman—had signed it with an 'X'. The date of purchase was 21 December, one day before Fred's final and fatal attack. Bell was alerted and he hurried to the shop. The chemist's description of his illiterate customer matched that of Charlotte Bryant, though he insisted that she hadn't used that name. He did remember her accent clearly, however: it was decidedly an Irish one.

But more proof was needed. The men from the Met invited the pharmacist to an identity parade. Charlotte Bryant and Lucy Ostler were summoned to appear in the line-up. However, the man failed to identify either woman as the purchaser of the can of Eureka weedkiller.

Bell was frustrated. He felt absolutely certain that Charlotte was the person he sought but could not yet, in police parlance, connect her with the crime. He had interviewed her, Detective-Sergeant Tapsell had interviewed her, the local police had interviewed her. All were convinced of her guilt. Yet all knew that the flimsy circumstantial evidence they had would be thrown out of court. They'd found the Eureka tin described by Lucy Ostler. There was a rubbish tip behind the Bryant cottage and there, among burnt and partially burnt debris, they found the tin. It was still recognizable as Eureka. An old coat was also found, belonging to a woman, and in one of the pockets traces of arsenic were detected.

Bell decided to talk to Charlotte again and, on 10 February 1936, went to interview her at the workhouse in Sturminster Newton. Flustered now, she tripped herself up many times, changing her story repeatedly. Bell felt he had enough to charge her with, and placed her under arrest.

She seemed to take it calmly enough, being concerned only for the welfare of her children. The police assured her that they'd be well taken care of.

———

It took four days to find her guilty as charged. Charlotte protested her innocence to the last, but it has to be said that she did not make a convincing defendant.

Her background was against her from the start. Though the trial took place not in Sherborne but in Dorchester—the town where she and Leonard Parsons had spent some of their last days together—her reputation had preceded her. Witness after witness—thirty in all—were prepared to lay bare her sins of the flesh and brand her a harlot. Leonard was asked whether he'd had sexual intercourse with her and he replied that he'd had it many times. The court was scandalized. In some eyes an adulterer—in particular a *female* adulterer—was almost as wicked as a murderer.

Yet the evidence that convicted her was wholly circumstantial. Nobody had actually seen Charlotte poison her husband. It could only be said that she'd been in the house at the time of his bouts of sickness.

Nor could it be proven that she was the woman who'd bought Eureka in Yeovil and signed for it with an 'X'.

The case for the prosecution rested to an extent on the finding of the woman's coat with traces of arsenic in the pocket. But Charlotte could demonstrate to the court that the coat didn't fit her, and denied it was hers.

They called two of her children to the stand. Ernest recalled how in December, following his father's death, his mother asked him to dispose of a number of blue-coloured glass bottles. Eleven-year-old Lily recalled how before this she'd seen Leonard Parsons with just such a blue bottle. He'd poured its contents onto a stone in Charlotte's presence and they had 'fizzed'.

Having deliberated for an hour, the twelve men of the jury found Charlotte guilty. Still she protested her innocence. When the judge passed the death sentence she broke down.

She frantically appealed the sentence but her appeal was dismissed on 24 June 1936.

She was hanged a little after eight on the morning of 15 July 1936 in the yard of Exeter prison by that practised hangman, Thomas Pierrepoint. Present also was her confessor, Father Barney, who described her fortitude on the scaffold as 'truly edifying'.

Was she really guilty? In view of the circumstances we might conclude 'yes', she was. Yet they are only circumstances. The fact that no other person known to Fred Bryant appears to have had motive or opportunity is convincing. Leonard was seen with the blue bottle whose contents fizzed but that was the hearsay of a child. He hardly stood to benefit from Fred's death; he was tired of Charlotte anyway.

We might well conclude then that she was the guilty party, yet she should have been allowed to appeal. A scientist who'd read about the case in a Sunday paper came forward to dispute some of the evidence but his findings were deemed inadmissible. The sentence was allowed to stand.

Regarding her treatment by the courts, the author Richard Clark makes an interesting comment, and it is this:

One wonders how much Charlotte's lowly status and acknowledged promiscuity played in the decision to neither reprieve her nor grant a new trial. Sadly Britain was very much a class-ridden society in 1936 and Charlotte was virtually at the bottom of the social pile—an illiterate, immoral slut. Were people like her simply expendable and their well-publicized executions considered as a good lesson to other women not to stray from the 'straight and narrow' paths of morality, as perceived by a male dominated society?

She was the second woman to be executed in England that year, the other being Dorothea Waddington. Posing as a nurse, the latter had given an overdose of morphine to two women in the nursing home she ran with her lover. Coincidentally, Dorothea was also the mother of five children. Unlike that of Charlotte Bryant, Dorothea's motive was profit. As it was, Charlotte left only five shillings and eight pence when she departed this life. Her children had to be placed in the care of Dorset County Council.

Shortly before her execution Charlotte had telegraphed a last-minute appeal to the monarch, begging him to 'have pity on your lowly afflicted subject'. King Edward elected not to involve the royal person on this occasion.

Leonard the gypsy would have had difficulty recognizing her on the day she ascended the scaffold—as would the men of the West Country who'd nicknamed her 'Black Bess'. The distress of the six weeks she'd spent in the condemned cell at Exeter, coupled with the prospect of her execution, had caused her once-dark hair to turn as white as a death shroud.

MARY SOMERVILLE, THE HEARTLESS GRANDMOTHER OF MONAGHAN

When the Roman Emperor Constantine converted to Christianity one of his first acts was to outlaw infanticide.

He did this not by making it a criminal offence, but by introducing two laws that he hoped would put an end to the practice. The first was perhaps the earliest form of child support in history. He decreed that public money be used to provide for couples who found themselves with more children than they could afford. Constantine reasoned that parents who could comfortably feed and clothe all their offspring would be less inclined to murder an unwanted baby at birth or soon after. The second act was as much an incentive to mercy as the first: anybody finding an abandoned infant and rearing it as his or her own could lay claim to all that infant's rights of property.

That Constantine found it necessary to legislate for the preservation of the lives of newborn babies is indicative of the widespread practice of child-murder in his day. From ancient times this offence was not punishable by law, except in Jewish and Christian communities. In lands such as India the custom of abandoning infants—especially female infants—endured until the British Raj called a halt to it. Only in recent times has China finally criminalized it.

In Ireland the situation was never clear-cut. Yet it's true to say that infanticide was widespread up until the 1960s. A glance at the court records of the nineteenth and early twentieth centuries shows the great number of women who were charged with this crime, known euphemistically as 'concealment of birth'. Indeed it was the most common serious crime with which women were charged.

Few women went to the gallows for it, however. This was due in part to the ambivalence of the Irish attitude to illegitimacy. By and large the shame brought upon a family by a daughter's giving birth to a bastard was considered a graver sin than the 'putting away' of the girl's newborn baby. In the eyes of the law, though, it was still classed as murder.

From the 1960s on, the incidence of infanticide decreased. There are those who contend that this drop was due to the availability of abortion in England. In 1967 that country legalized the termination of a pregnancy, inducing an increasing number of Irishwomen to cross the water and abort their unwanted foetuses. Whatever the truth of this, it is a fact that in all countries of the world where abortion is illegal the rate of infanticide is highest. There was the contraceptive pill too. Though not generally available in Ireland until much later, it could be procured easily enough—and doubtless led to fewer unwanted children, potential victims of infanticide.

In 1949 a curious thing happened. This was the year in which the Twenty-Six Counties became the Republic of Ireland. With the passing of new legislation through Dáil Éireann, infanticide stopped being categorized as murder, should the victim be under the age of twelve months. It was still a felony, but ranked now alongside manslaughter, thus no longer a capital offence.

One section of the Act is interesting in light of the case that follows. It reads:

A woman shall be guilty of felony, namely, infanticide if—
(a) by any wilful act or omission she causes the death of her child,
being a child under the age of twelve months, and

(b) the circumstances are such that, but for this section, the act or omission would have amounted to murder, and

(c) at the time of the act or omission the balance of her mind was disturbed by reason of her not having fully recovered from the effect of giving birth to the child or by reason of the effect of lactation consequent upon the birth of the child and may for that offence be tried and punished as for manslaughter.

Mary Somerville was unfortunate on two counts. One: she killed an infant in 1938, eleven years prior to the passing of the new law. Two: the child was not her own. It belonged to her daughter Annie.

About the first of August, 1937, I was in Monaghan Town and met Robert Harvison there. He escorted me out the road towards my home. When we were at Sheetrim, Harvison and I lay down on the ground by the side of the road. He pulled down my knickers, put his private part into mine and had connection with me. He then walked along with me to my mother's house.

Thus did Annie Somerville describe her initial sexual contact with the man who was to father her baby. She was seventeen at the time.

Annie was born in 1920 to a woman who herself was the victim of several unlucky 'connections' in her youth. Mary Somerville was born in Glasslough Street in the town of Monaghan in 1887. Her parents were poor; the Latimers were one of several socially and economically disadvantaged members of the Church of Ireland in the town. Though her father William was a bailiff and earning a good wage, he drank most of his salary, leaving his wife to cope as best she could. As a result, Mary didn't have much of a start in life.

Her education was rudimentary and at the age of twelve she went into domestic service. She was an unattractive, ungainly girl who found herself shouldering more of the work than was her due. She also found herself the object of the attentions of a young kitchen boy. He made her pregnant and she became a mother at the age of thirteen. The child, a boy, was given up for adoption.

In 1905 she met a widower, John Somerville, who was forty-eight at the time—thirty years Mary's senior. They married all the same, and she moved into his farm at Knockaturley, a townland close to Monaghan. The couple had seven children, four boys and three girls. In 1937 the eldest daughter was living in Northern Ireland, married to a man with the curious Dickensian name of Magwood. Six siblings remained at the farm. The youngest, Eliza Jane, was eight; the eldest girl, Annie, was eighteen.

Mary Somerville had a difficult time of it. She'd lost her husband to tuberculosis in 1930 and was thrown on the mercy of charitable organizations. It was either that or the poorhouse, and no self-respecting mother would choose *that* for her children. The charity came in the form of assistance from the County Monaghan Protestant Orphan Aid Society, who generously gave the widow £38. It was no great sum but neither was it as paltry as it might seem now; in the 1930s in rural Ireland a farm labourer was paid on average fifteen shillings a week.

The little family got by. Mary worked hard, making the most of the few acres and livestock left to her when her husband died. Her oldest son William also worked the farm, as well as earning extra money labouring for local farmers. Likewise, Annie and the younger children earned their keep with work on their own property and temporary domestic service in the homes of others.

By our standards the Somervilles lived in absolute squalor, in conditions to rival the most wretched country in the developing world. But in the late 1930s Ireland was a developing country too, almost completely dependent on Britain for its trade. America's Depression, begun in 1929, had spread to the rest of the world, hitting Irish farmers badly. Markets for grain were drying up; herds had to be drastically reduced in size. The Somerville farmhouse was a small cottage with a corrugated-iron roof. There was a kitchen on the ground floor and one bedroom. The two rooms upstairs were barely habitable and were used by the boys in summer as bedrooms. We can only hazard a guess as to how they managed throughout the rest of the year.

Yet to the casual observer the family—apart from their poverty—would have seemed relatively normal for the time: a widow and her children making do in the absence of their dead father. Except that Mary's dead husband had fathered only two of the children; each of the other five was the offspring of a different man. Mary was, then, in the eyes of the neighbouring community, a loose woman—presumably the men who'd fathered her children were of loose morals as well but this appears to have gone unrecorded. Be that as it may, Mary was shunned as a moral degenerate, and her children were considered to be no better. To add fuel to the local gossip, the eldest daughter Martha—now Mrs Magwood—had given birth to an illegitimate child in 1934. Mary Somerville had had to rear it while her wayward daughter was getting settled with her husband. At age fifty she had, understandably, her fill of children about the place.

It's perhaps for the above reasons that the neighbours kept a close watch on the Somervilles, on the girls especially. When the second eldest, Annie, became pregnant by the young philanderer Robert Harvison, a boy she'd met in Sunday school, the neighbours watched and observed the course of the pregnancy, scandalized that the girl seemed to be following in her mother's footsteps.

On 11 July 1938 a workman passing by the cottage saw Annie in the yard and it was clear that her belly was no longer distended with the child she'd been carrying. She'd given birth, then.

In the days that followed, however, Annie was frequently seen sunning herself in the yard or engaged in some minor chore. But the house was strangely silent. There was no sign of the baby. An inquisitive neighbour or two called on Mrs Somerville on some pretext or other and noted that Annie, though clearly lactating, seemed to have no infant to breastfeed. They neither saw nor heard the child.

In the end the suspicions deepened to such an extent that it was decided to involve the Gardaí. Sergeant Michael Cahill of

Monaghan police station called to the farm with a body of officers to interview the family. All strenuously denied that a child had even been born in the cottage. But the sergeant persevered, quizzing Annie over and over again. She finally broke down and confessed. Yes, she'd given birth to a baby daughter shortly after sunrise on Monday, 11 July.

'And where is this child now, Annie?' asked the sergeant.

'My mother took her away.'

'Did she now? And when did this happen?'

'About ten minutes after the baby was born,' Annie confessed.

Sergeant Cahill turned his attention on the mother. Up until now Mary Somerville had stoutly denied that any child had been born to her daughter. But she could hardly keep up the pretence, not when all the evidence, and Annie's admission, contradicted her story.

She conceded at last that the child had been born on the day in question and at the time stated. She'd been ashamed of her daughter's immoral conduct, she said, and had immediately brought the infant to Belfast, thinking to give it into the care of an old friend, Mrs Wilson.

Sergeant Cahill suspected she was lying. He described her as being of 'a rough masculine type, and appears to be below the average in intelligence'. Nor did she appear to care at all for what the neighbours thought—and told him so in coarse terms.

He decided to detain her. In the ordinary run of events the Gardaí would have done no such thing without sufficient evidence that a felony had taken place. Cahill was concerned though that, what with the border so close by, Mary might decide to skip across and thus be out of his jurisdiction. He brought her to the station in Monaghan.

He was glad that he did so because a phone call to Belfast revealed that the address Mary had given him as that of the foster mother—13 Murdock Street—didn't exist. Nor was there a Mrs Wilson residing anywhere in the area. He had no choice but to lock her up for the night.

The next morning she confessed.

'The child isn't in Belfast at all,' she told him.

'Ah. Where is it then, Mrs Somerville?'
'I put it in a well out at the house.'

———

They found the tiny body in the place that Mary described. It was a well, no more than a shallow pool of water five feet below the surface. It lay about sixty yards from the Somerville cottage, close to a public road.

The pathetic remains were that of a baby girl, newborn with the umbilical cord still intact. Somebody had wrapped the infant in a cloth and placed it in a cheap multicoloured shopping bag, then weighted it with three heavy stones. It was a sorry sight and the police officers were greatly upset by it.

In the morgue the remains were examined by a local surgeon and a dispensary doctor. Both confirmed what Sergeant Cahill suspected and feared: that the baby girl had been born alive, but had died of drowning. Mary Somerville had deliberately and callously taken away her daughter's newborn baby and disposed of it like an unwanted litter of puppies.

Cahill listened gravely as Mary confessed her guilt. Garda Patrick McGillion banged out her statement on the keys of the heavy-duty Underwood typewriter. It was short:

On Monday, the eleventh of July 1938, about 3 am, my daughter Annie Somerville, aged seventeen years and eight months, gave birth to a baby girl in my house. The child was born in a bedroom. I attended at the birth. My four children also my granddaughter were sleeping in the room at the time. About fifteen minutes after the child was born I took it to the kitchen. The child was crying in the kitchen. It was in a shopping bag lying on a couch. About daybreak I took the child up to a deep hole of water about sixty yards from the house, put two or three stones on top of the child in the bag, and dropped it into the water. I did not look at the child when I was carrying it up to the hole of water and I could not say if it was then alive. The bag containing the child's body sank in the water and I did not see it since. I have heard this statement read and it is true.

The statement is signed in a shaky, almost childlike, hand—the signature of a woman who could barely write her own name, never mind read a typed document.

When the case came to trial at the Central Criminal Court in Dublin on 15 November—justice was served quickly in those days—Mary Somerville made a poor showing in the dock.

First, though, the hunt was on for the young man who was the father of the dead child. Annie confessed to her dalliances with the farm labourer Robert Harvison, who was only fifteen at the time of his first 'connection' with the girl, that fateful hot evening of July 1937 when they'd lain down together by the side of a country road.

Robert and she had made love frequently after that—twice a week, according to Annie, up until the middle of December. By that time their 'connecting' was taking place indoors, in his father's barn. By that time, too, Annie knew for definite what she'd suspected for a month or more: she was carrying Robert's child. She vowed to stop their sex.

'I told Harvison that I would not allow him to have connection with me any more,' she stated, 'and no other man except Robert Harvison had connection with me at any time.'

Robert was arrested and charged with 'unlawful carnal knowledge', a serious enough charge at the time. With the prospect of a prison sentence hanging over him he wriggled like a sandworm on a fish-hook, pleading his innocence and denouncing the young girl he'd made pregnant.

'I never done any harm to any girl I went with,' he swore. 'There was plenty of fellows with her forby me.'

Superintendent O'Reilly of the Monaghan Gardaí took a dim view of Harvison's slander. 'It is interesting to observe the apparent simplicity with which the girl was seduced and the unrepentant attitude and youth of the seducer,' he wrote. 'It is an interesting commentary of itself of [sic] the type of people involved.'

Nonetheless the lad was acquitted when his case came up before Justice Sheehy in Monaghan Circuit Court. Apparently Annie had given a false statement. Initially she'd said that Robert first had 'connection' with her in July 1937, but in the Circuit Court she'd changed this to October. Her unreliable testimony was enough to allow the charge against him to be dropped.

Mary Somerville did not fare so well in the Dublin courtroom. She was found guilty of the wilful murder of her daughter's newborn baby.

In his address to the jury the judge was scathing of an attempt by her counsel to defend Mary's actions. Mr Hooper had spoken of the shame brought upon any family by the birth of an illegitimate child. The judge understood this very well. What made him angry was Hooper's contention that the shame was 'a natural thing to try to avoid'.

'Gentlemen,' his lordship thundered, 'I don't quite follow what is meant by that sentence! It may be a natural thing to try to hide the birth of an illegitimate child, but it is not suggested that it is a natural thing to *kill* for the purpose of hiding its birth.'

It was at this point that Mary's fate was sealed. This was no 'concealment of birth', according to the judge, but the murder of a human being—and they must treat it as such.

'One hears a good deal of discussion from time to time about child murder,' he went on, 'but let me tell you that the life of a young child is just as sacred in the eyes of our law as the life of an adult person, and the life of the child is protected by our law in just the same way as the life of an adult person. And why should it not be?'

A reasonable question. Yet a mere eleven years following the judge's deliberation the state was taking a different view. Infanticide was not murder if a judge did not choose to see it as such. The Act of 1949 would leave the way open for much 'concealment of birth'.

Mary Somerville had killed too early. On her would therefore fall the full rigour of the law. She was sentenced to be hanged.

Mr Hooper appealed and the appeal was heard. Her sentence was commuted—to penal servitude for life, as harsh a sentence as one could imagine. She served it out in full and died in prison, a broken woman.

Her eldest son Edward took over the running of the little farm in Knockturley. Her local minister wished to have her youngest children removed to an institution but in the event they all stayed on at the farm, as was Mary's fervent wish.

Annie married a local farmer and gave birth to four more children.

BRIDGET WATERS: REVENGE OF A WOMAN SCORNED

It was 12 March 1944 and the war was in its final year. It was going badly for the Germans. Hitler had overreached himself, as Churchill had predicted he would. He'd opened up too many fronts in his mad bid to take over the world. The Allies reckoned that now was the time to strike where Hitler had left himself most vulnerable: close to home, in France. The Normandy invasion, code-named Operation Overlord, was about to be put into effect.

It had to be kept top secret of course, and Hitler had his spies everywhere, in Ireland especially. For it is a shameful fact that although Éamon de Valera had declared the nation neutral, some Irish wartime sympathies lay with Germany. Not that the Irish particularly liked the Germans and their bellicose empire-building—far from it. It was for some political extremists a case of remembering Wolfe Tone's credo: 'England's difficulty is Ireland's opportunity.' My enemy's enemy is my friend.

On Sunday, 12 March, renegade Irishman William Joyce, aka 'Lord Haw-Haw', was telling the listening world that a German victory was nigh. In his plummy, mock-aristocratic tones he was urging his fellow countrymen to hitch their wagon to the rising star of fascism. Churchill's war cabinet were in no doubt that, were news of the invasion to leak out, Ireland would be a likely source. They therefore banned all travel between Britain and her supposedly neutral neighbour.

Among the many whose plans were thus upset was Bridget McCluskey, a twenty-four-year-old Irish nurse working in Liverpool. A Dublin girl, she'd left home at seventeen to be employed as a nanny in Lewes, Sussex. In 1940 the War Office had conscripted hundreds of young women like her for nursing duty; they sent her to Merseyside. She'd planned on celebrating St Patrick's Day with her family and friends and now her hopes were dashed. So she did the next best thing: in the company of a group of fellow nurses she took the train to London on Wednesday. They booked into a small hotel and prepared to have a good time the coming weekend.

There wasn't a lot to celebrate that Friday. Britain was sick of war and nearly five years of rationing. For the young people either serving at the front or helping the war effort at home, a night on the town was a matter of finding your way through streets lit only by glimmer lights and people carrying torches. There were no neon signs advertizing the entertainment venues, but blacked-out windows and only jazz music to guide you to your destination. You knocked on doors to be admitted to pubs and clubs that resembled the American speakeasy of a previous decade.

Once inside, a girl might think she really had stepped into a little piece of the USA. The music was American, thanks to the Glen Miller influence; the British had learned to drink American 'cocktails', and the place might have more GI and USAF airmen per cubic foot than Madison Square Garden.

It was inevitable then that Bridget, slim, pretty and green eyed, should catch the attention of an American. He wasn't a soldier, sailor or airman, though. Frank Knowlton Waters, thirty-six, was a civil engineer working for the US-owned Boeing aircraft company. He was earning good money, and determined to spend it that St Patrick's night. He was delighted too to find a real, live Irish girl to spend it on.

He knew she was Irish because she was dressed in a flashy green silk blouse and skirt. She even wore a sprig of shamrock at her breast. ('It wasn't really shamrock at all,' Bridget confided later. 'It was just some old clover I picked in Hyde Park, but of course Frank didn't know the difference.')

It was the start to a whirlwind romance, with no time lost between the first date and the tying of the knot—by no means unusual for those dangerous times when men went off to war leaving behind a bride with confetti still sticking to the soles of her shoes. Frank and Bridget spent the weekend together in the country, and married the following Saturday in Cheshire. It was 25 March and they'd known each other barely nine days.

So fast did their love-affair progress that Frank's letters to his parents crossed in the post. The first they were aware of the new woman in his life was when she'd already become Mrs Waters. She was 'new' because Frank had only recently recovered from the death of his fiancée, a childhood sweetheart from Los Angeles, killed in a freak road accident. He'd told Bridget nothing about her, determined to start with a clean slate. The next letter the astonished parents received was dated the previous Monday. In it Frank enthused rapturously about the lovely 'Irish colleen' he'd met in London and fallen in love with, and whom he planned to marry as soon as possible. Mr and Mrs Waters had misgivings.

'So soon?' Martha Waters said on learning the news. 'Why, he can hardly know the girl. It's a rebound marriage. He was probably so lonely.'

Bridget for her part was delighted. At a time when so many available men were away fighting for their country, it was hard for young women to find a worthwhile suitor. You made do or you decided to wait out the war. But the war, thought in 1939 to be over by Christmas, looked set to drag on for another five years unless something drastic was done. And so it was that when Frank Waters—American and therefore synonymous in the Irish mind with prosperity—proposed marriage, Bridget jumped at the chance. She saw herself in California, with a beach house in Malibu and sunshine all year round. American men had a good reputation too for being kind and generous. Frank was intelligent and charming, with a good education. He was ready to resume his law studies and enter a lucrative legal practice when the war was over. What more could a single Irishwoman of modest background want?

By chance Frank's company sent him to Liverpool for a time, to oversee the construction of a yet-to-be-tested aircraft component. Bridget accompanied him with pleasure. It gave her an opportunity to show off her 'catch' to her former colleagues at the hospital. She was not the only war bride of course. Several others had married just as hastily. The difference was that those women's husbands had either returned to the front or were awaiting the call-up. Those young women faced the appalling prospect of early widowhood. Not so Bridget; Frank Waters was a non-combatant. Assuming he wasn't killed in an air-raid, he'd most likely survive the war.

Frank was posted back to London towards the end of May. Perhaps he knew of the impending allied invasion of France on 6 June but, if he did, he would have been under the strictest of orders not to share the information with his wife—his *Irish* wife. Bridget knew only that her husband worked for Boeing. He did not tell her that his work was on the B-17 bomber, the so-called Flying Fortress that since 1943 had carried out hundreds of daring daylight raids on Germany. Prior to 6 June Frank's military employer, the 457th Bomb Group, was stationed in the south of England. Now plans were being drawn up to transfer some of the operations to northern France and to Paris, once the country was freed.

It was, and D-Day entered the history books. In the third week of June, Frank was sent across the Channel to assist in the push to Berlin. His group were flying more than five hundred sorties a month. This time Bridget wasn't allowed to accompany him.

It was also around this time that she confirmed what she'd suspected: she was pregnant. Her one wish was that the baby would be born on American soil. She had high hopes that it would. All England was rejoicing at the turn-around that the Normandy landings had achieved. The end of the war was in sight. The Americans would be going home soon.

The news came out of the blue. A genuine bombshell could hardly have been more devastating. Frank wrote to Bridget from Paris, telling her that he'd had second thoughts, that in his opinion their marriage 'was a mistake'. Kind and generous Frank had turned out to be a rat.

No amount of frantic correspondence from Bridget could budge him. And the most hurtful part was that she didn't know the reason behind this sudden change of heart. She wondered if the prospect of fatherhood scared him, but he seemed too mature and responsible for that to be the case. Bridget of course was unaware of Frank's dead fiancée but from all accounts she played no part either. Had he met another woman in France? He swore to her that he had not. It was baffling.

Bridget, looking forward as she'd done to the three of them celebrating Christmas together—Frank, herself and the baby, due at the end of November—now faced the prospect of giving birth alone. She considered returning to Dublin but the shame would have been too great to bear. She even considered going to France and confronting Frank. The problem was that the US Air Force refused to give her his exact address. And she had no money of her own.

In due course the baby was born: a boy, and Bridget named him Frank. If she thought that this gesture might change her husband's mind then she was wrong. He wrote back to say that he'd no intention of living with her again. The truth emerged: Frank was a womanizer. He was having such a good time in Paris, he said. He even boasted of his conquests. He did promise, however, to send $50 each month as maintenance for Bridget and Frank junior.

Despite her anguish at her husband's unfeeling behaviour and selfishness, Bridget continued to write, continued to hold out hope of reconciliation. Only twice did she receive the promised $50 a month; then it dried up, leaving her practically penniless. To add insult to injury, in autumn the following year, when the war was over, Frank returned to the United States without even telling her. The next Bridget heard, he was living in Las Vegas and working as a cashier in a bank. Worse still, he had initiated divorce proceedings.

Bridget saw red. She was determined that philandering, feckless Frank Waters wasn't going to get away with it. He might think he could treat another woman in this shabby way, but not Bridget McCluskey. She was going to show the American that she wasn't to be trifled with.

The first thing she did was to take her case to the Married Women's Association (MWA). Founded in 1938, the association had come into its own during the war, when so many British women shared Bridget's predicament. 'Marry in haste, repent at leisure' seemed to apply to scores of war brides. The MWA sought a fairer deal for married women in which family finances were better distributed. They also wanted better legislation for children, and the right of the mother to share the marital home. Broadly speaking the association was agitating for the equality of women. As such it was years ahead of its time.

The MWA very generously paid for Bridget to fly to Las Vegas with her child, that she might confront her callous husband. But perhaps better than financial aid was the press publicity they set in train. They were determined that Bridget make a test case on behalf of so many young women who'd been abandoned by American husbands. Compared to the situation in Britain, the US legal system made divorce easy—and many would say *too* easy.

Until changes to the legislation took effect in the 1960s, British law as applied to divorce was a bad joke. If a couple wished to divorce, at least one had to sue the other, and a 'co-respondent' had to be involved, i.e. a person who had an extramarital liaison with one of the parties. The usual course adopted was to arrange for the husband to fake a tryst in a seedy hotel. A prostitute would be paid a fee to join him. The pair would then be photographed *in flagrante delicto* and this 'evidence' of adultery presented as grounds for divorce. In the US it only needed one party (the husband) to sue, on the grounds that the marriage had been a mistake.

The MWA wished for Bridget to be the first British war bride to contest such an unfair divorce action. They therefore had her flown to America. She arrived in New York City on 13 April 1946, in a blaze of publicity. All the main US papers had been alerted to her coming, and there were also radio interviews lined up.

Pretty Bridget Waters was the darling of the American press. With young Frank in her arms, her outspokenness and her flashing green eyes, she had the reporters eating out of her hand. They'd never seen anything like her.

'I'm the first British war bride to arrive here to contest a husband's divorce action,' she announced. 'There's more of us on the way. A lot more.'

She explained how so many women were, like her, receiving divorce papers in the post. It was the coward's way, she said, and she wasn't having it.

'We're not taking it sitting down,' she warned. 'If I win this case it will give the Married Women's Association a lot of encouragement.'

'What about Mr Waters?' somebody asked. 'What does he say?' She snorted.

'Frank says he made a mistake,' she answered angrily. 'Well, if he made a mistake then he's bloody well about to pay for it!'

She went on to state that neither of them, Frank especially, had a right to say that the marriage was 'a mistake' before giving it a proper chance.

'The baby has a right to know his father,' she said. 'He has a stake in this marriage too.' She lowered her voice. 'Frank never wanted that baby. He wanted me to have an abortion.'

The reporters were writing furiously.

'Do you still love him, Bridget?' one asked presently, and she claimed she did. In almost the next breath, however, she was denouncing him as a scoundrel.

'Frank hasn't seen the baby or given me a penny!' she cried. 'Well, he can't get rid of me that easily. He promised me fifty dollars a month and little Frank and I are going to get it. Even if I don't get a pound out of it, the fight will do me good!'

It was good copy and the journalists were revelling in it. One suggested that Frank might have had a change of heart. Perhaps if he knew she was here in the United States he'd think differently. Would she care to telephone him collect?

But Frank refused to accept the charges. The reporters assured Bridget that their papers would be happy to pay for the call. The long-distance operator put her through.

He was none too pleased to hear from her, not even when she lifted tiny Frank up to the phone so that he could coo a hello to his father. In the end, and very grudgingly, he agreed to meet her at the airport in Boulder City, Nevada, near Las Vegas. He put them up in a tourist cabin he'd rented.

The reunion had one unexpected outcome: Frank fell in love at once with the little boy he'd never seen. But for the most part his resolve remained unshaken. He wanted a divorce. Bridget vowed that he'd get one only after a court battle. She filed a countersuit. Already she was learning how things were done in America. . . .

———

Frank Waters never had a chance. From the moment he took the stand in the courtroom the jury was against him. It was 27 April 1946; the place was Las Vegas, the sitting was the District Court and the judge was Alfred S Henderson.

If the jury members took an instant dislike to Frank then his pretty wife had them worshipping at her shrine. They loved her. They listened raptly and sympathetically as in a low voice she told her tale of desertion.

In no time at all they reached their decision, and it went entirely against Frank Waters. They decided that he'd failed to support his wife, had deserted her and treated her with 'an unusual degree of mental cruelty'. They awarded Bridget custody of the child, a decision that surprised no one. But they also ordered Frank to pay $60 per month to Bridget and $40 to the baby. Moreover, there was to be a payment of 'arrears': a sum of $1000.

Justice had been done. Bridget had her doubts though. What, she wondered, was to prevent Frank reneging on the arrangement? Were she to take the next plane back to England, who was going to ensure that Frank would keep up the payments?

It was a valid argument, and one to which no one could give a satisfactory answer. She also considered $100 a month too little for herself and the child to live on. So she made the decision to remain in Las Vegas and find a job to augment her income. In an era that preceded strict immigration laws and 'green cards', this proved surprisingly easy. Within days Bridget was putting her wartime nursing skills to good use at the Clark County General Hospital in Las Vegas. She and Frank junior took lodgings in the home of a Mr and Mrs Biggs.

In the days to come their relationship was understandably strained. But not impossibly so. Frank became the doting father—as so many men will do when given the chance of parenthood without responsibility. He came to see his son as often as he could, bringing him little gifts and playing with him.

He showed little interest in Bridget herself, though. Only on one occasion did he take her on an outing, to Mount Charleston, a local beauty spot and tourist attraction. She knew he only did it for the child; nonetheless she felt that she might still be able to engineer a change of heart. To this end she visited Frank's mother in Los Angeles.

Bridget was not well received. In fact she was treated like 'an unwelcome stranger'. It was evident that Frank had poisoned his parents' minds about his wife. She did, however, pick up a little clue to Frank's behaviour towards her. Martha Waters let slip that her son might be having an affair with another woman.

By this time—August 1946—Bridget was becoming accustomed to the American way of doing business. She was making friends in Las Vegas, paying the odd visit to the casinos and trying her luck on the gaming machines. Her female colleagues at the hospital introduced her to the seedier side of life in the gambling city, bringing her along when they went out on the town. Little Frank could stay behind in the care of her kindly landlady, Mrs Biggs.

During the course of one such girls' night out, Bridget broke down in tears. She told the women that her husband might be two-timing her. It wasn't that he was 'playing the field', she said. She feared that Frank was in another long-term relationship. If that were the case then all was lost.

'You need a detective, honey,' somebody said. 'You should pay some guys a few bucks to follow the bastard and find out for sure.'

She reached into her handbag and slid something across the table. Bridget picked it up. It was a miniature revolver, a four-shot .22, so tiny that Bridget could conceal it in her palm.

'You can borrow it,' her friend said. 'You might need it in case of prowlers.'

_____

Bridget had no difficulty finding a detective agency. Las Vegas was awash with them: firms ready and willing to chase up bad gambling debts, investigate newcomers to town on behalf of the casino bosses—and keep tabs on errant husbands and wives. She engaged the services of Hiram McClure and Harry Oatman.

What the private eyes uncovered shocked her. In the letters he'd sent from France her husband had bragged about his womanizing. Here in Las Vegas he'd apparently had a string of girlfriends. Now he seemed to have embarked on a serious affair with Lucille Robinson, the divorced daughter of his landlady.

All this should have been enough to damn Frank for ever in Bridget's eyes. What really made her seethe with rage, though, was that he'd had sex with Lucille in the very tourist cabin he'd rented for her and the baby. Not once, but several times, according to McClure and Oatman.

She was still smarting on Labour Day, 2 September, when Frank arrived at the Biggs's home to collect Frank junior, now ten months old. He was to take the child on an outing, something he did three times a week. Bridget opened the door.

All might have been well that day had Frank come alone. He might have lived to a ripe old age in the healthy desert air of Nevada. But he came that day with a passenger, and parked his car close enough to the house to afford Bridget a clear enough view of her. It was Lucille Robinson, the woman who'd taken her place in Frank's affections. To compound her heartbreak and sense of abandonment, Bridget saw that the private detectives had played down Lucille's looks: she was an extremely attractive woman.

Or so Bridget thought.

She left Frank standing at the door, which was unusual. She always invited him in. He started talking about divorce again; he hadn't mentioned it since the court case.

'So what about Lucille?' Bridget asked.

'Where did you hear about her?'

Bridget peered again at the woman in the car. She was blonde and well dressed. It was hard to tell her age.

'I heard about her ten days ago,' she told Frank, 'and I haven't slept since. Do you want a divorce because of Mrs Robinson?'

He must have wondered how she'd found out. He hadn't told her a thing.

'Yes, she had something to do with it,' he conceded. 'Were you spying on me?'

He was angry. Bridget would later describe him as 'vicious and frightening'. But we have only her word to go on. She claimed that he made a threatening move towards her, then stopped.

She panicked. She went into the bedroom where little Frank was in his playpen. She picked him up and wrapped him in a blanket.

A blanket. It's well to remember that the date was 2 September. In Las Vegas at that time of year the daytime temperature averages 32°C (about 90°F), a degree of heat that most of us will experience only on a holiday in the tropics. A blanket would have been the last thing that the ten-month-old child needed.

But Bridget did. Before picking up little Frank she'd gone to the drawer where she kept the miniature revolver she'd borrowed, for protection against 'prowlers'. Clutching it in her left hand, she wrapped part of the blanket around it. Only then did she pick up her child.

We cannot say with certainty that she intended to kill Frank, but she did intend to do him some injury. Tiny though the .22 was, it was still lethal at close range. According to her version of events, Frank went slightly crazy. He tried to take his son from her.

'Don't you dare touch the baby!' she cried.

But the baby was precisely the reason Frank had come to the house, as he did every Monday, Wednesday and Saturday. He couldn't understand his wife's reluctance to allow him to have the boy now.

Again, we have only Bridget's word to go on. She claimed that Frank told her he was taking the infant away from her, to where 'you won't see him again'.

That was when he snatched the boy from her, and that was when the gun 'went off'. Next she knew, Frank was lying bleeding to death in the doorway and the child was wailing in fear, and seemed to be in pain as well. . . .

Bridget would recall the next few seconds only with difficulty. Her husband lay dying, unconscious; she was holding a smoking gun. The child was sitting on the floor beside his father's body. Bridget saw an angry red mark on his knee; with horror she watched blood oozing from it. The bullet that felled Frank must have grazed her son. She dropped the revolver and went to pick him up, frantic with worry.

At that moment a blonde woman appeared at the open door. Seeing her silhouetted against the harsh sunlight of Nevada, Bridget mistook her for the hated Lucille Robinson. Only when the woman bent down over Frank's motionless body did she realize her error. It was Mrs Maude Griffiths, Lucille's mother.

Bridget phoned the police herself. The first officers on the scene took stock of the situation and decided that the sobbing young woman with the green eyes was no threat to anyone. One of them examined little Frank and called for an ambulance. He was brought to Clark County Hospital.

For Frank Waters senior it was too late. The bullet had pierced his heart. In all likelihood he'd died within seconds.

Bridget didn't deny pulling the trigger.

An everyday scene in a slum area of Liverpool in the 1880s.
Catherine Clifford and her sister Margaret would have
lived in similar circumstances.

Liverpool slum area, 1895. A ragged couple share a
pipe in a doorway.

St Patrick's Cathedral, Armagh. Bellina Prior lived with her
family on Vicar's Hill, facing onto the grounds of St Patrick's.
HULTON/GETTY

Bustling Market Square, Armagh, in the 1880s.
NATIONAL LIBRARY OF IRELAND

A car is stopped by soldiers with bayonets during the Irish Civil War. The murder of farmer's wife Margaret O'Sullivan in 1923 would have barely registered outside her home-town of Killorglin, because of the large number of war casualties at the time.

Kerry in 1923. Soldiers look on as a crane lifts derailed train carriages back onto the tracks during the Civil War.

FATAL FACILITY; OR, POISONS FOR THE ASKING.

Buying poison over the counter in a chemist's shop. Bridie Walsh was able to purchase from a pharmacist the strychnine that she used to poison her husband, Michael Walsh.

Charlotte Bryant, nicknamed 'Black Bess', was convicted in 1936 of poisoning her husband, Fred Bryant, with arsenic.

A tin of Eureka weedkiller is compared with the tin, found destroyed at the Bryant farm, which was used to poison Fred Bryant.

Fred Bryant was serving as a military policeman in Derry when
he met Charlotte in 1922.

Glaslough Street in Monaghan, where Mary Somerville
was born in 1887.

Bridget Waters with her baby son, Frank,
at the US Embassy in 1946.
HULTON/GETTY

Bridget with her son, held by Glen Bodell, investigator for the
defence, during a break in her trial in Las Vegas for the
murder of her husband.
TOPFOTO

'I shot him,' she told Inspector Charles Morrison over and over. 'I was afraid he might injure the baby.'

———

Even before the trial opened in Las Vegas, Bridget Waters was making headline news. The people of the desert city were moved when the story emerged. They took Bridget's side and raised more than $1000 towards her defence costs. She was treated with great leniency and understanding by the authorities as well. They gave her the run of the Las Vegas prison where she was held on remand, and allowed her to visit little Frank in the hospital where his knee injury was being treated.

It might seem a little odd to us that Americans in both New York and Nevada should have lavished compassion and help on an Irishwoman, a stranger to their shores, whose only link with their country was her hasty marriage to Frank Waters. The fact is that at the close of the war America was experiencing an unusual qualm of conscience for the suffering of the nations of Europe. This applied not only to their wartime allies, Britain and France, but Germany too. US troops had returned with eyewitness accounts of a devastated continent, of women and children reduced to begging by the roadside, and worse.

There were those too who regretted their nation not having waded in sooner, when Germany overran so many countries and threatened so many more. It was only when the Japanese attacked Pearl Harbor on 7 December 1941 that the US was finally galvanized into action. Had they moved sooner then the war would surely have been shortened considerably. There was therefore a feeling of guilt across the country, and a desire to make up for the foot-dragging. In 1947 the Marshall Plan was put into operation. It had the twin effect of placing a buffer before the spread of communism while helping Europe rebuild itself.

And so it was that when Bridget landed in New York, the Americans were delighted with yet another opportunity to put things right. Many saw Frank Waters as an embarrassment. There are those who believe that—for this very reason—justice was not done, that emotional considerations overrode fair play, and a murderer was treated with undue leniency.

Whatever the case, Bridget's trial was the talk of Las Vegas long before it was called into session. When it opened on 20 October 1946—after a number of delays—gamblers, cowboys, hookers, and the simply curious, all crowded into the courtroom to hear the plucky Irishwoman tell her story. Judge Henderson had heard some of it before: he'd also presided over her divorce trial.

Her defence lawyers pleaded an 'insane fear for her child's safety' as her motive for shooting Frank Waters. Bridget was, from the very beginning, from St Patrick's Day 1944, an innocent young woman who'd been treated disgracefully.

But the District Attorney, V Gray Gubler, bent over backwards to paint an altogether different picture. The defendant, he claimed, was not the loving wife and mother she was made out to be. And he had the letters to prove it: letters written to the murdered man during his sojourn in Paris, and letters Frank wrote to his mother, as well as to another confidante, the fabulously named Crystal Waters, his aunt in New York City.

'The difference between us,' he wrote on 7 October 1944, 'came up when Bridget expressed her unwillingness to come to London to live with me. She preferred staying in Liverpool to joining me, because her friends were there.'

She joined him eventually, but according to Frank she went on to go out twice with a British sailor. When he protested, they had a row, she called him all the names under the sun, and returned to Liverpool. He followed her there and they ironed out their differences. She again joined him in London.

'Then after about a week her true nature asserted itself,' Frank told his aunt. 'She became abusive and sarcastic. She condemned me, my country, its customs, etc.'

At this point the district attorney paused, letting the words sink in. There are few more patriotic peoples than the Americans. In the immediate aftermath of the war they were especially so, and unusually sensitive to any criticism of their country. It wasn't looking good for Bridget. And there was more.

'At first I had friends out to the house,' Frank confided to Aunt Crystal. 'With them she was violently argumentative and she humiliated me in front of them.'

A short time later she was pregnant. According to the deceased she was furious when she found out. She would 'not then, or ever' have the baby, she told him, and ordered him to look for an abortionist. He failed to find one. Her anger grew. So 'vicious' did she become that in the end he had to tell her to pack her bags and go.

By this time the jury were already pencilling her in for the gas chamber. District Attorney Gubler pressed home his advantage, and picked up another letter.

'Convinced that I meant business,' Frank had written, 'Bridget began to recant, said she wanted the baby. I told her I didn't believe her and she began to get desperate. One night she tried to commit suicide. She loaded a hypodermic syringe with poison. I tried to get the syringe away from her. She screamed she was losing her mind.'

Bridget had been pale on entering the courtroom. Now she looked ashen. There was no doubt that Frank had written those words because before they could be entered as evidence she'd been asked to verify that the letters were his. Prior to the trial she'd had no idea that Frank had been so, well, *frank* with his aunt in New York. Whether he'd been telling her the truth was of course another matter entirely. For the moment though it seemed as if all was going the prosecution's way. Frank's letter continued.

Of course I capitulated and she returned to normal. I began to suspect she had been faking and I cooled off. And again she put on the act, took half a grain of morphine. The result was that I capitulated again. I was more convinced than ever she was faking. In the meantime, she became more sure of me and began to talk of the abortion again on the grounds that having a baby would be inconvenient. I agreed, but for some other reasons.

So now I'm waiting for developments. If she gets an abortion I will consider myself free. If she has a baby I won't know whether she wanted it or had it because she couldn't get an operation. In either case, I don't know whether I owe the marriage another try or not. At the moment I don't think it would ever work. What do you think?

As if Frank's words from beyond the grave weren't damning enough, Gubler had another ace to play: the gun that killed him. He handed it to the judge, who inspected it with interest before returning it. Gubler held it aloft for the jury's benefit.

Its size seemed to belie its deadliness. What was even more surprising though, according to the district attorney, was the fact that significant force was needed to pull the trigger. Bridget had repeatedly told both police investigators and court that it 'just went off', that Frank's shooting was an unfortunate accident. Gubler was stating that this was highly unlikely. Bridget intended to kill her husband and applied sufficient pressure to the trigger to send a bullet straight into his heart from close range.

But if the district attorney thought he could convince the jury with his words then he was mistaken. He was a big man and the tiny weapon looked tinier still in his hand—like a child's toy. And, like a child's toy, it could be harmful if the person holding it wasn't used to firearms, as Bridget was not.

Gubler should have known that, from the start, he was fighting an uphill battle. When the trial ended and the verdict was given, the jury members, unanimously, confessed that it had never been their intention to find the young Irish mother guilty of murder in the first degree. At the end of the four days they returned a verdict of involuntary manslaughter. They sincerely believed that Frank Waters died because a mother was trying to protect her infant.

Judge Henderson displayed an equal degree of mercy. He sentenced her to 'one to five years' in prison. None believed that she'd ever serve the longer term. Bridget herself told reporters that she considered the trial a fair one, that she was satisfied with the verdict. Her only regret was that she'd be parted from her son.

In the event she served eighteen months. She was paroled on 3 May 1948 and deported to England, together with Frank junior. The boy had been in the care of foster parents in Carson City since the start of her incarceration. He was three by this time and had known his mother only as a woman who lived in a grey institution and somebody he visited several times a week. Bridget hoped that those bleak memories would fade from the lad's mind in time.

A happy ending then. And yet the case throws up some disturbing questions concerning the impartiality of American justice. From the moment Bridget set foot in the USA she was widely seen as the innocent party, the wronged woman. She was what we'd call today a media celebrity. She was young, she was pretty, she was engaging—how could she possibly be capable of wickedness?

When her case came to trial it was almost a foregone conclusion that the law would go easy on her. The proceedings commanded far more news coverage than a relatively 'minor' shooting such as this would normally receive. Not only the State of Nevada but the entire United States were eagerly awaiting the outcome. Had the city of Las Vegas sent her to the gas chamber there'd have been a public outcry.

Let us deviate for a moment and contrast her crime and punishment with those of John Kramer, convicted four years earlier—by the same State of Nevada—of murdering his girlfriend. Kramer, a native of Pennsylvania, was a coalminer by trade. He shot Frances Jones, the woman he'd known and loved for fifteen years. He was in love with her but she'd consistently refused to marry him. He got drunk on 15 February 1940 and shot her dead. He was so drunk, he claimed, that he could hardly remember the incident, and he was stricken with remorse. Nevertheless he died in the gas chamber, convicted of pre-meditated murder.

The difference between John Kramer and Bridget Waters is that Kramer was a very plain man of sixty-one. Those who knew him described him as 'gentle and kind'. And he loved Frances Jones dearly. He almost certainly didn't plan to kill her.

Bridget on the other hand had lied continually, not only about the killing but also about the events following her marriage to Frank.

The jury at her murder trial would have read the reports of her divorce trial. At one stage this 'loving mother' had been prepared to accept $6000 from Frank in exchange for the baby. In effect she was selling little Frank to his father.

The private detectives she'd hired to investigate Frank's indiscretions were called to testify. Bridget had asked if they could 'push him off the cliff', were they to find him with another woman at Boulder Dam. McClure had told her he was a detective, not a member of 'Murder Incorporated'.

She'd also borrowed the gun. She was unused to handling a firearm, so why did she immediately reach for it when her husband—and not a prowler—was supposedly threatening her and her child? She wasn't blind drunk at the time, as John Kramer had been. Nor was she temporarily insane, as her defence tried unsuccessfully to establish.

It's hard to ignore the possibility, then, that Bridget Waters escaped her just punishment simply by the grace of her sex, her age, and her green-eyed good looks.

MARIAN PRICE, THE WOMAN WHO KNEW NO COMPROMISE

L ife would be so uncomplicated if terrorism were simply a matter of the good guys versus the bad guys. We'd be able to continue branding as 'monsters' and 'psychopaths' those who use time bombs and other sneak methods of destruction against members of the public.

Terrorism, though, is a loaded term. The IRA can point out that their members who bombed civilian targets in Northern Ireland and England were not so very different from the French resistance, the *maquis*, who did much the same in German-occupied France during WWII. The *maquis* were not only greatly admired by the British, they received British aid and training too. What was the difference? France was occupied by the Nazis, the north of Ireland by the British.

And yet there's something very cowardly about warfare that's waged by covertly planting a bomb, retiring to safety and waiting for it to explode. It's a dirty business in wartime, but even dirtier when war has not been formally declared, and civilians—children especially—are killed or injured in the blast. Few people can afford any sympathy for a bomber.

Marian Price will probably go to her grave still believing that bombing is justified. That the device detonated by remote control, or the ticking time bomb, are acceptable weapons. As recently as 2000 she was still asserting as much. 'Bombs are legitimate weapons of war,' she told the *Guardian*, 'and the IRA used them against an occupying force. The IRA campaign was never about killing civilians. That was not our intention, but accidents happen. That is an unfortunate consequence of war.'

It doesn't seem to have occurred to Marian that she was arrested in 1973 for deliberately placing bombs on the crowded streets of central London. In 1973 there was a strong military presence in Belfast, her home-town, but sightings of soldiers were extremely rare in the English capital. She could argue that she and her co-conspirators were targeting buildings important to the forces of the Crown, and that was indeed the case. The targets were New Scotland Yard, the Old Bailey, the Army Recruiting Office in Whitehall, and the British Forces Broadcasting Office in Westminster. But only the last two housed military personnel.

The IRA telephoned through a one-hour warning. Two of the car-bombs—at police headquarters and at the radio station—were defused before they could be activated. The others exploded outside the court buildings and the recruiting office. A public house, The George, that minutes before had been crowded with customers, was wrecked completely.

In the event, more than two hundred people—all non-combatants—were maimed in the blasts. One man, a fifty-eight-year-old caretaker named Fred Milton, died of heart failure as a result of the terrorists' handiwork. He happened to be walking past the court buildings at the time of the explosion. Eyewitnesses said later that it was a miracle the death toll wasn't higher.

Among the casualties were ten police officers. On receiving the IRA warning of the impending explosions, the policemen were engaged in shepherding the civilians to safety. It was a ghastly precursor to the Omagh bombing. On 15 August 1998 police officers were likewise conducting members of the public away from the danger zone—or so they thought. In reality they were herding them straight into the vicinity of the car containing the bomb.

No wonder eyebrows were raised when more than twenty years later, in the wake of the Omagh carnage, one of the apologists for the culprits turned out to be Marian Price. She'd become a spokesperson for the 32-County Sovereignty Committee, the political wing of the Real IRA, the republican terror group responsible for the bomb that claimed twenty-nine innocent lives. Many were asking themselves what sort of woman Marian was. What, they wondered, does it take to become a ruthless bomber?

———

It might surprise those people to learn that Marian Price had always wanted to be a nurse: a carer and a healer. That she chose what amounted to a diametrically opposed 'career' owed much to where she came from. She and her sister Dolours grew up in Andersonstown, a working-class area of Belfast to the south of the Falls Road.

Some would say that bombing was in the girls' genes. The sisters were of staunch republican stock, of a family that had strong links to the IRA. Both mother and father were enthusiastic 'volunteers' in the 1930s, when the organization was particularly active—as was their aunt, Bridie Dolan. In 1938 she was blinded and lost both her hands while moving a cache of IRA hand grenades from one house to another.

For the most part, though, life was relatively uneventful in the succeeding decades for nationalists living in Belfast. The armed struggle for a united Ireland was largely at an end. Apart from the odd isolated incident there was no IRA activity to speak of, and certainly no concerted campaign.

Three important issues were to change all that: the attack on the civil rights marchers at Burntollet Bridge in 1969, internment, and the Bloody Sunday massacre. At the time of the mass shootings in Derry on 30 January 1972, Dolours Price was eighteen, her sister two years younger.

It was the second issue, however, that was to impact most on the Price sisters. The internment of nationalists without trial drove many young people across Northern Ireland into the recruiting offices of the IRA. There were few homes in Andersonstown that did not have at least one male member of the household behind bars in one of several prisons, including the notorious Long Kesh, and the Maze with its H-Block. Reports were getting out about wholesale torture of internees, Amnesty International and the United Nations were demanding explanations of the British Government—and nationalist Belfast was seething at the crass injustice of it all. It would be February 2005 before the British Government, under the Freedom of Information Act, admitted that 'deep' interrogation of internees —including 'hooding, wall standing, subjecting to noise, deprivation of food and sleep'—was a common occurrence during the internment years.

That internment was unjust (and illegal under international law) could not be disputed at the time, but only in hindsight did those responsible for its introduction and implementation appreciate the beast they'd unleashed in 1971. Reginald Maudling was British Home Secretary at the time. He would write, twenty years later, what amounted to an admission of failure by his government.

> *No one could be certain what would be the consequences [of internment], yet the question was simply this: what other measures could be taken. Today, with hindsight, it is clear how awful the consequences were. The experience of internment from 1971 to 1975, was by universal consent a mitigated disaster which has left an indelible mark on the history of Northern Ireland. It is hardly surprising that every administration since then has recoiled from the idea of repeating the tactic.*

He went on to deplore the casual brutality displayed by the military during and after arrests. The late Eamon Collins, murdered by dissident republicans in January 1999, described just how brutal such arrests could be. He was guilty of nothing when the soldiers came to his parents' home, and he leaves us in no doubt that this and subsequent outrages induced him—a peace-loving young man—to join the republican movement.

Two of them grabbed me, one on each shoulder, and ran me back up the avenue towards the house. I could smell drink on their breath. As we got to the turn at the top they began to beat me with their rifle butts. Others appeared and started to kick and punch me all over my body. 'Get your fucking hands on your head, you Irish cunt. Get your legs out. Get your fucking legs out.' They kicked my legs further and further apart until I fell to the ground. They spreadeagled me in the dirt. I tried to keep absolutely still, but from the corner of my eye I could see several soldiers at the front door. They kicked the door again and again until it gave way. They rushed inside and soon I heard my mother, who had been crippled with rheumatism for years, screaming from her bedroom window upstairs. A soldier walked over to me and shoved his SLR rifle in my mouth, cracking my front left tooth. I could feel the cold of the steel upon my tongue as he shoved the barrel right to the back of my throat. I remember the taste of the gun oil. I began to choke. 'I'd blow your brains out for tuppence, you rotten Irish cunt.' . . .

John and my father went into the first jeep, while I got into the second. They told me to lie on the floor as three soldiers got in on either side of me. They began to hit me with their rifle butts on my arms, legs, back and buttocks. I could hear my mother screaming hysterically. One of my guards shouted, 'Fuck off you old whore!' as the jeeps drove off. During the journey the soldiers spat on my head continuously. I felt a hand move up my trouser leg to pull hairs off my calf. All the time they kicked me in the ribs on both sides of my body. One soldier pulled me by the hair and began to bang my forehead against the radio on the floor of the jeep. A rifle barrel was twisted around the area of my anus, then two of them put their guns to my head, clicked off the safety-catches and ordered me to sing 'The Sash' . . . which I sang as best I could while they beat time with their rifles on my back. I felt these drunken madmen were capable of anything.

The galling thing for the nationalist population was that such savagery was reserved only for them. At least at first. Reginald

Maudling saw internment as a means 'to prop up an ailing Unionist government'.

For more than a year no loyalists were rounded up, while republicans were held in leaky Nissen huts. On the outside the death toll rose alarmingly while riots and street disturbances became worse. Thousands moved home. Alienation rose sharply in the Catholic population.

Nowhere was this alienation felt more than in the Price family. In 1972 a brother and two uncles were 'behind the wire'. Men were being 'lifted' by day and night, rounded up and interned seemingly at random. The injustice they saw all about them was to send Dolours and Marian into the arms of the IRA. And thus it was that in June 1972 they were at the gates of Long Kesh internment camp, to welcome republicans released back into the community. Among those prisoners was a young man named Gerry Adams. By the end of 1972 the sisters were in training as terror activists, learning among other skills the deadly craft of bomb-making.

On leaving secondary school Marian had begun a nursing course at the Royal Hospital near the Falls Road. As time went by, however, she was running into difficulties. Junior nurses were expected to take up residence in the nurses' quarters at the hospital. Marian's clandestine night-time activities with the IRA were making this increasingly impossible. She decided to train as a teacher instead and enrolled at a Belfast college. She was eighteen; Dolours was twenty-one. One year later she was in London in the company of ten others—young people like herself, fired with an almost fanatical desire to attack the British establishment, to bring to the very heart of the Empire the same level of violence that its soldiers had visited on her people.

The group was made up of Belfast volunteers and were the first such 'active service unit' the Provisional IRA would send to England. By 1973 the 'Provos' had become the dominant republican grouping, eclipsing the power and stature of the Official IRA. Marian's unit included her sister Dolours and one Gerry Kelly, now a leading light in Sinn Féin and a fervent supporter of the peace process in Northern Ireland. It's been claimed that the Price sisters actually commanded the unit but this has never been properly established. At this remove, and given the secretive nature of the organization in question, it probably never will be.

The plan was to enter Britain by water and to leave by air. By the time the bombs went off in London the eleven conspirators would be in a plane over the Irish Sea and making the approach to Belfast. The unexpectedness of the attack would, it was reasoned, catch the British with their pants down. In the ensuing pandemonium the authorities would try to seal the ports and other escape routes, but it would be too late. The focus of investigation would be England, not Ireland.

The *Daily Mail* newspaper took the call at around two in the afternoon. At first the woman on the switchboard was highly sceptical, suspecting a hoax call. Until Dolours Price uttered a code word that was used by the IRA in Ulster in just such circumstances. The operator reached into a drawer of her desk and took out a small notebook, one that should be opened only in an emergency. Sure enough, the codes matched.

The call went through to Scotland Yard. London was on high alert. They had one hour in which to render four bombs inactive.

But Marian and her group had reckoned without the efficiency of the combined forces of the London Metropolitan Police and fifteen others. Within minutes two of the car-bombs had been located and defused. At Heathrow Airport, just as the eleven were set to board a plane out of London, the police pounced. Only one member escaped. The rest were arrested and taken into custody. The time was approaching 3 pm.

Marian refused to speak while in custody, as was her right according to the law of the land. As she waited for the officers from the Met to arrive she looked at her watch. It was 3 pm, the time the bombs were primed to explode. She smiled. That smile was to cost her dear.

———

All were sentenced to life imprisonment. The group were split up and sent to different prisons. Marian and her sister, together with Hugh Feeney and Gerry Kelly, were taken to Brixton jail.

They refused to be treated as ordinary criminals and demanded that they serve their sentences in Northern Ireland. From a compassionate viewpoint the latter wasn't unreasonable: friends and family who wished to visit them in jail would otherwise have to incur the expense of a plane or boat journey.

Both demands were rejected. The climate in England by this time was strongly anti-republican. Most felt that the men and women who'd deliberately tried to kill and maim ordinary British subjects going about their business in London deserved no special favours. Among those who took a hard line was the prime minister, Margaret Thatcher. The Price sisters could put up or shut up.

Marian and the others were undeterred. If the British Government weren't prepared to accede to their demands then the prisoners would go on hunger strike until they got their way—that is, if death didn't intervene.

'I have dedicated my life to a cause,' Marian declared, 'and because of that I'm prepared to die.'

She had a number of illustrious examples to follow. Since Thomas Ashe, who died in a Mountjoy jail in 1917, the hunger strike had been an effective republican device. It lent the striker victim status and—more effective still—it could focus the attention of the wider world on his or her cause. There was always the possibility too that the striker might die, in which case victimization would become martyrdom.

In December the Provisional IRA kidnapped the German industrialist Thomas Niedermayer from his home in west Belfast. Their ransom terms: his life in return for the transferral to Northern Ireland prisons of Marian and Dolours, along with the eight other prisoners. In January the German Chancellor, Willy Brandt, pleaded with the British premier Edward Heath to accede to the IRA demands. Heath turned him down, refusing to 'deal with terrorists'. The Irish Government backed Heath's position, and Niedermayer 'disappeared', his dead body not being discovered until 1980. He'd died of a heart attack while being held against his will.

The British authorities were more aware than anybody of the propaganda coup that the deaths in prison of Marian and the others would represent. Hardly into the second week of the strike, the four were already commanding international publicity. This was the last thing Thatcher needed. Internment without trial, RUC sectarianism and brutality, trigger-happy soldiers, and the shockwaves produced by Bloody Sunday, were combining to paint a most unflattering picture of Britain and the situation in its Irish dominion.

Gerry Kelly, Hugh Feeney and the Prices were into the forty-sixth day of their strike. A danger point had been reached. In the past, few hunger strikers had survived much beyond the fiftieth day. The Home Office gave orders that the prisoners be forcibly fed.

The horror began on 13 December 1973 and went on for a total of one hundred and sixty-six days. This is how a reporter for the American paper the *Irish People* described the ordeal endured by the four. It is not for the squeamish. Even more harrowing is the thought that Marian and her fellow protestors suffered this barbarousness every day for a little over five months.

Having a disgusting gruel pumped into one's stomach isn't only uncomfortable, but extremely painful. As part of the protest, the four refused to eat or cooperate with the forced feedings; therefore, they had to be subdued each time and their mouths forced open. This was accomplished through brute force or the nose was pinched shut and, when the victim gasped for air, an instrument or piece of wood, etc. was shoved between the teeth and the mouth was pried open. Pliers and clamps were variously devised to get the job done by applying pressure on the jaw. A plastic tube, too large in diameter for comfort, was then quickly rammed down the throat and into the stomach. A nutrient substance was poured or pumped through it.

Often the procedure had to be done several times to get it down the right pipe, so to speak, which insured that whatever lubricant was used had wiped off. Frequently, the victim vomited everything up and the procedure would begin again.

Then, naturally, the Brits figured a way around all this jaw and throat messiness—down through the nose. This orifice is particularly unsuited for plastic pipes being jammed into it. . . .

Hugh Feeney, who spent time in America working for the Republican movement after his release from prison in the early 1990s . . . said that it was s.o.p. [standard operating procedure] that if he vomited up the mixture, which was very common as the process was extremely uncomfortable and unnatural, they would re-pump his vomit back into him. Often the tube shoved into his nose wasn't lubricated at all and was purposely angled to rip into the tender cartilage. Even if everything stayed down as planned, the stomach was so over-filled with the liquid that he could hardly walk, crawling on his hands and knees into his cell almost wishing he were dead.

In short it was the sort of torture we usually associate with the world's most repressive and nastiest regimes, and it was to shame Britain for a long time after. Margaret Thatcher had scored a spectacular own goal.

The sisters became the darlings of the media. Their courage touched the hardest of hearts. Marian's letters home were avidly reproduced in nationalist newspapers in Ireland and abroad. It was evident that she and her sister were no common, bloodthirsty psychopaths but intelligent and—yes—sensitive human beings. Dolours was even writing poetry:

> *And I could say such things to you*
> *Could tell you of my dreams,*
> *How once there was a little girl*
> *Who danced in summer streams,*
> *And sat upon a mountain,*
> *And thought she was God,*
> *Knowing in her innocence,*
> *All wrongs that she must solve*
> *Then I could show the woman*

Marian Price (right) and her sister Dolours, at a civil rights
demonstration outside Belfast, 1970s.
TOPFOTO/PA/EMPICS

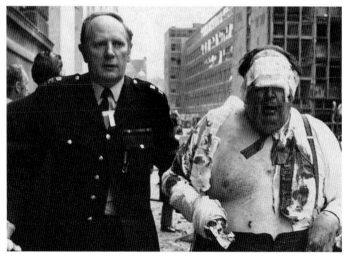

A policeman helps a barrister, injured in the IRA bombing
of the Old Bailey in London, 1973.
HULTON-DEUTSCH/CORBIS

Two of the alleged IRA bombers in the back of a prison van.
They were arrested at Heathrow Airport while trying
to leave the country.
HULTON/GETTY

Garda Michael Reynolds, shot while unarmed by bank robbers
Marie and Noel Murray in St Anne's Park, Clontarf, 1975.
COURTESY OF THE IRISH TIMES

Police searching the murder scene in St Anne's Park, where
Garda Michael Reynolds was shot.
COURTESY OF THE IRISH TIMES

The funeral procession for Garda Michael Reynolds.

Norma Cotter received a life sentence for the murder of her husband, Gary Cotter, in 1995. She appealed, and walked free after a new trial in 2003.

Gary Cotter, murdered by his wife Norma with the shotgun she had given to him as a Christmas present.

Anna Maria Sacco.
DEREK SPEIRS

Franco Sacco earned his living by running a chip shop in
Rathfarnham, one of a chain of takeaways owned
by his father-in-law, Luigi Sacco.
DEREK SPEIRS

Joe McDonnell, a corporal in the Royal Irish Regiment, was fatally wounded after being stabbed with a kitchen knife by his wife, Karen McDonnell, in 1997.

Lorraine Farrell committed suicide after killing her lover,
Paddy Farrell, with a shotgun in 1997.

Julie McGinley, who with the help of her lover, Michael
Monaghan, murdered her husband, Gerry McGinley,
while he was sleeping. His body was discovered,
buried in a shallow grave, in 2001.

Michael Monaghan, sentenced to life imprisonment for murdering the husband of his lover, Julie McGinley.

ALAN LEWIS/PHOTOPRESS BELFAST

Dolores O'Neill killed her husband, Declan O'Neill, in 2002 with a plumber's hammer and carving knife, after enduring years of domestic violence. She was convicted of manslaughter in 2004 and sentenced to eight years in prison.

COLLINS PHOTO AGENCY

Still so much the child
Who knows to hold your hand in hers,
If only for a while
And would you gladly give yourself
To one who soon may die . . . .

The issue of force-feeding a prisoner who's on hunger strike is a vexed one and a legal minefield. On the one hand the prison authority has a responsibility towards those committed into its custody; it cannot allow their lives to be placed in jeopardy. But it also has a moral obligation to respect the rights and wishes of a prisoner, including the person's right to refuse food and drink.

In the end the Price sisters, through their lawyers, mounted a legal challenge to the forcible feeding. Their case rested on whether the Home Office had the right to resort to such means where refusal of nutrition did not arise 'from a medical or psychiatric condition'. The debate was heated. But they won, thereby setting a precedent that was to affect the lives of the republican hunger strikers who came after them, notably Bobby Sands and his fellow prisoners, ten of whom starved themselves to death in 1981.

The sisters' victory secured their release from their British prison on 18 March 1975, a little over two years after the Old Bailey bombing. They were transferred to Armagh jail where they were allowed to serve out the rest of their sentences as political prisoners. The cruelty that had accompanied their incarceration in England had been emotional as well. On learning that their mother was dying of cancer they'd requested compassionate leave to see her. They were refused. Nor were they permitted to attend her funeral. She died one month before their transfer 'home'.

It was many years before Marian and Dolours recovered from their ordeal—and it's perhaps in doubt that they ever fully recovered in an emotional sense. In any event both developed tuberculosis while in Armagh, and Marian almost died of anorexia. At one stage she weighed only five stone and ten pounds.

They were granted their freedom in 1980, Marian through her

brush with death having secured for them the Royal Prerogative of Mercy.

In 1983, ten years after the Old Bailey bombing, Dolours married the film actor Stephen Rea, perhaps best known for the starring role in *The Crying Game*. Although a Protestant, the Ulsterman has never been reluctant to voice his sympathies for the nationalist cause.

Marian Price still makes the news bulletins on occasion. On 20 January 2000 the United States immigration authorities turned down her visa application. She claimed it was because of her bitter opposition to the Good Friday Agreement. She long ago lost all faith in the Provos, the men and women whose cause she once served with such fervour. For her the Provisional IRA have become no more than 'an armed militia of the British'.

It's unlikely though that she ever will be allowed to enter America, now or in the foreseeable future. The terrorist attacks of 11 September 2001 put paid to her chances of doing so. The last thing America wants is an unreconstructed bomber and terrorist, and that is how Marian Price, in some quarters at least, will for ever be regarded.

ELIZABETH DOUGLAS, THE SANDY ROW EXECUTIONER

Law before Violence

MOTTO OF THE ULSTER DEFENCE ASSOCIATION

This is the story of another terrorist from Northern Ireland. But, unlike Marian Price, she gained no widespread notoriety. She never planted a bomb; nor did she go on hunger strike. It's unlikely too that she ever used—or even held—a firearm. Unlike Marian Price, Elizabeth Douglas is virtually unknown to anybody outside Northern Ireland. Even to those in her native city of Belfast her name is no more than a minor footnote to the history of the Troubles. This is the story of a terrorist from the other side of the sectarian divide, of a woman who grew up in the belief that the people of her own working-class area were somehow 'the enemy' of another working-class people: those who went to a different church of a Sunday and sang different songs down the pub of a Friday night. This is a story about power, and how power placed in the hands of the wrong person will invariably be abused. Lastly this is a story of how a political cause can deteriorate into gangsterism and mob rule.

The Ulster Defence Association is the largest Unionist terrorist organization in the North. Formed as a Protestant retort to the IRA, it succeeded in murdering more than five hundred Catholics since its founding in 1971, yet it was only in 1991 that the British

Government declared it illegal—effectively providing yet another example of the curious logic that pervades the politics of Ulster.

The UDA had its heyday in 1972 when its membership reached 40,000, yet it was in 1974 that it was at its most murderous. On 17 May it perpetrated the worst atrocity of the 'Troubles' when it exploded four bombs in the Irish Republic, one in Monaghan and three in Dublin city. Thirty-three died and over two hundred were maimed. The UDA admitted responsibility.

Almost from the time of its founding in 1971 observers had sensed that society was dealing with an organization far more sinister than most Irish republican groups, both mainstream and splinter. A press release that followed the wanton and unprovoked slaughter of those innocent men, women and children confirmed this fear. Sammy Smyth, who represented both the UDA and a workers' strike committee, issued a horrific statement.

'I am very happy about the bombings in Dublin,' he wrote. 'There is a war with the Free State and now we are laughing at them.'

Laughing at them. The IRA bombers had always claimed to regret any loss of innocent life—distinguishing as they did between 'soft' and 'hard' targets, the latter being the forces of the Crown and Unionist terrorists. And it must have come as a surprise to the citizens of the 'Free State' that their country was at war with its northern neighbour. In July of that same year it would emerge that the UDA was indeed a truly terrifying body, and that several of its female adherents would support Kipling's claim that in some cases a woman can be 'more deadly than the male'.

On 29 July workmen came upon the corpse of a woman in a ditch close to the M1 motorway, at a point where it lets into south Belfast. The main road gives on to a roundabout leading to Stockman's Lane, which in turn connects to the city's prosperous Malone Road. The woman had been battered to death. The grisly find might seem shocking to us now in the early years of a new century but in 1974, in Northern Ireland, it was simply a case of one more victim of a campaign of hatred; the 1970s were witness to the ferocious 'tit for tat' killings that had made the city as dangerous as Beirut.

This isolated death barely merited a mention in the annals of the Troubles, occurring as it did in a month that saw more 'high-profile' mayhem. The IRA detonated bombs in Manchester and Birmingham on 14 July; miraculously no one was killed or injured. Not so when the same terrorist group bombed the Tower of London three days later, killing one person and maiming forty-one others. On Wednesday, 24 July, a nationalist councillor was abducted in County Tyrone; his body was found in a lake a month later. He'd been shot several times, allegedly by members of the Ulster Defence Regiment, a wing of the British Army cobbled together from an older regiment and remnants of the discredited B-Specials.

By coincidence a young woman named Ann Ogilby had also disappeared on 24 July. And like the missing councillor she too was a native of Tyrone. She was born and reared in Sion Mills, a picturesque village that lies about three miles from the town of Strabane and some five miles from the Donegal border. Architecturally speaking it's an unusual place: practically all its fine buildings were designed by William Unsworth, a son-in-law of the founding fathers who built two linen mills on the river that runs through it. Ann Ogilby spent her childhood in one of the old terraced millworkers' cottages. Her family were poor Protestants who found it difficult to raise their thirteen children in Sion Hill. The once-prosperous village had seen its decline with the closure of the mills in the early 1960s.

When she was seventeen Ann went to Belfast in search of work, glad to accept whatever was offered her: a succession of low-paid positions in shops and offices. She was a very attractive girl with dark-brown silky hair and blue eyes, the kind of girl who invited second looks and much male attention.

Perhaps it was her stunning looks that led to her downfall. It seems that, almost from the beginning, she began a slide down the social ladder in the city, falling in with a progressively worse crowd. In her quest for Mister Right she embarked on a number of ill-fated love affairs, none of which lasted any length of time.

She began to drift, losing one job after another, being evicted for being behind with the rent.

Ann was sexually active all the while and producing children. She shared the belief of naïve young women that having a man's child will automatically 'bind' him to a relationship. Six years following her arrival in Belfast she'd given birth to four children, each by a different partner. But at last she appeared to have found a decent man. In August 1972 a friend introduced her to William Young. He was married but the marriage was 'on the rocks'. According to William, his divorce hadn't 'come through yet'. He claimed to have fallen in love with pretty Ann Ogilby, and she fervently believed that she was in love with him. The pair set up house together.

But Young was not what he seemed; over the course of time Ann discovered that her live-in lover was deeply involved with the UDA. He was arrested in 1973 and sent to the Maze prison, County Down. No charges were formally brought against him—but there was no need. The government's policy of internment without trial was still being implemented, despite talk of its being phased out. This emergency measure, introduced largely for the apprehension and confinement of republican factions, could be, and was, used against 'loyalists' too, much to their disgust. Indeed the imprisonment of its members was a fierce bone of contention among UDA men—and heaven help anyone who did or said anything that would exacerbate the position of a man locked up in the infamous Maze.

Ulster's loyalists, moreover, prided themselves on their loyalty to one another. Should a member of a Protestant terror group find himself behind bars for an extended period then he could almost automatically call on the support of his comrades. The UDA were no exception. Moneys were collected on a regular basis and a portion of these was used to buy food and other items to make a stay in jail tolerable.

The difficulty arose when the UDA mistakenly assumed that Young and his wife were still living together. In actual fact they'd been estranged for over a year. Nevertheless Mrs Young was given food parcels to pass on to him. But they never reached him—or so Ann Ogilby claimed.

Ann was incensed. She found herself practically destitute while her partner languished in prison. She'd lost the home she'd made with her partner and was now reduced to living at the YWCA hostel on Malone Road. She had four children to support, as well as looking after William Young. She was providing food parcels entirely on her own account. It wasn't fair.

Unfortunately she made the deadly error of airing her grievances to anybody who'd listen—and one of those listeners had the ear of Mrs Young, who in her turn was a good friend of Elizabeth Douglas.

The Ulster Defence Association prided itself on being run along military lines. Its founders had divided loyalist Belfast into companies: A-Company, B-Company, C-Company and so on. Each controlled a section of the city, and each had its officers, all complete with military-style ranks. The organization also ran its membership according to strict military codes. There were rules to be obeyed, and anybody caught breaking them was punished—often savagely.

All ranks were answerable to the company 'commander', Andy Tyrie, who as a rule ran a tight ship. So too did the 'commander' of the women's branch of the UDA: forty-year-old Elizabeth Douglas. She kept the female 'troops' in line and you crossed her at your peril. When she gave an order you obeyed it at once, without question. It was harsh, yes, but in those harsh times strict rules and stiff penalties for breaking them were needed for survival.

Elizabeth listened to the allegations made against Ann Ogilby. They were serious. She ordered that Ann be brought in for 'questioning'.

Poor Ann. She knew so little about this terror organization that was so much a part of her lover's life. It seems likely that she in her naïvety misunderstood how important was the role of the UDA in Protestant ghettoes like Sandy Row. Elizabeth Douglas might have appeared to Ann as being a somewhat overweight and plain middle-aged woman, indistinguishable from so many such women who frequented the loyalist bars at the weekend. Women who drank their G&Ts and sang lustily along to kick-the-pope anthems like *I'll Always be a Womble*:

Oh I'll always be a Womble
till the day I drop and die,
And I'd hate to be a Fenian
'cause they're bastards and they're sly.
Oh they're all dirty wee fat fucks
and they're two-faced slimy cunts,
They should be burnt out and sent to Dublin
to spend their fuckin' punts.

Ann couldn't have known that she was dealing with a woman who loved power above all else. Elizabeth Douglas had never had much of it, having grown up as the middle daughter in a poor, working-class family. She married when she was seventeen and in 1974 was the mother of four grown-up children. All she'd seen of life was the drudgery of marriage and motherhood during a time when Ulsterwomen lagged behind their sisters in Britain, who from the 1960s on were starting to assert themselves.

If the Troubles in the North produced anything at all it was a group of men and women, both nationalist and unionist, who suddenly found themselves in powerful positions—as leaders—a situation that would have been unthinkable in peacetime. Shrewd observers believe that the violence in Northern Ireland was deliberately prolonged by such people, who were concerned that in the event of a ceasefire they'd find their power taken away as quickly as it had been given them.

When Ann Ogilby crossed Elizabeth's path, the UDA woman had a police record to rival that of any criminal, male or female. She'd been in front of the judges and magistrates for a list of offences that included forgery, smuggling, assault and actual bodily harm. She'd also helped her husband run a brothel.

If Ann Ogilby's first mistake was to bad-mouth William Young's wife, her second was to make a caustic remark about the UDA within earshot of Elizabeth Douglas. That would happen after her interrogation.

She was picked up on the evening of 23 July and brought to Elizabeth's home in City Street. They asked her questions. Had she really made disparaging comments about Mrs Young? Ann admitted that she had. Elizabeth tore strips off her, threatening her with dire consequences and ostracization if she did anything like that again.

'We have rules, here,' she said. 'We all stick to them and I expect anybody new to do the same.'

Ann said nothing, but seemed to be shocked into silence by the seriousness with which Elizabeth Douglas regarded the situation. And she was still angry, continuing to see herself as the wronged party.

But she promised to behave and they brought her to Glengall Street bus station beside the Opera House so that she could take a bus back to the hostel. There were nine women besides Ann, all squeezed into the one car. Ann boarded the bus and said goodnight to two of her 'minders'. She said a little too much for her own good.

'Who does she think she is?' she asked, referring to Elizabeth Douglas. 'The Queen?'

The 'commander' was furious. She issued a curt order and, before the startled eyes of bus driver and passengers, a woman walked out in front of the vehicle, preventing it from moving off. Three other women boarded the bus, dragged Ann from her seat and bundled her back into the car they'd come in. It sped off with a squeal of tyres.

What probably saved Ann's life that night was a phone call made by one of the bus-station staff. He took down the number of the car before it was driven away, and alerted the police. A bulletin was sent out and the car stopped on Malone Road. The RUC constables were surprised to find so many women jammed into the one vehicle.

'We're off to a party, love,' one said with a wink. 'You won't report us for a wee bit of overcrowding now, will you?'

But the policeman told them of the report he'd received about one of their number being dragged off a bus.

'That would be me,' Ann Ogilby volunteered, perhaps attempting to ingratiate herself with Elizabeth Douglas. 'It was nothing. Only a couple of us fooling around.'

The police weren't convinced, however, and all were escorted to Queen Street RUC station. Statements were taken. Ann Ogilby was noticeably distressed, but refused to make a complaint, even when pressed. No charges were brought, though the women were held until 2 am. Their names and addresses were taken. All lived in the Sandy Row area.

The police invited Ann to return to the station the following day, to make a statement. Again she refused. She asked to be driven to the Social Services Centre in Lower Crescent. She had an appointment there, she said.

She failed to keep the appointment, scheduled for three o'clock that afternoon. By nightfall she'd be dead.

———

What happened that evening in Sandy Row is shocking. And all the more because those involved were not only female but some as young as sixteen and seventeen. Perhaps it's an indictment of any society if it allows its children to become so brutalized that killing another human being is considered to be all in a day's work.

At 1 pm a group of UDA women met in a bar in Sandy Row to discuss the Ann Ogilby situation. One was Elizabeth Douglas, another Kathleen Whitla, her 'second-in-command'. Alcohol was drunk freely and the talk was of the impossible situation the 'renegade' had placed them in. No one knew whether the police had quizzed Ann yet and, if so, what she'd let slip about the organization. Elizabeth said that 'something would need to be done'. They moved on to a second public house and at about 2 pm, Elizabeth had made her decision. The loose cannon would have to be brought in.

Ann Ogilby failed to keep her appointment that day because a man driving a blue van came for her at the YWCA. We know the van was blue because that is what Ann's eldest daughter, six-year-old Sharlene, reported later to the police. We also know that the man was twenty-five-year-old Albert Graham, known to his friends as 'Bumper'.

Mother and daughter were driven to a building in Hunter Street, close to Sandy Row. It was a disused bakery serving as a clubhouse for the UDA. Ann had already been there on a number of occasions; William Young had brought her. She'd enjoyed the company of the men and women; there'd been a real sense of camaraderie, of 'us against the Fenians'. Now the atmosphere was suddenly sinister.

Bumper unlocked the front door, and escorted Ann and Sharlene inside. To their great surprise a group of women wearing face masks appeared as if from nowhere. Elizabeth Douglas, wearing no disguise of any kind, joined them. Her words left Ann Ogilby in no doubt that she'd crossed a line as far as the UDA were concerned.

'Take her upstairs,' Elizabeth told the women, 'and give her a good rompering.'

What was meant by this emerged when all concerned were brought to trial. Three masked women had frogmarched the prisoner to a room on the first floor. Sure enough, it was used mainly as a children's 'romper' room or playroom. It is hard to imagine less appropriate surroundings for what was to ensue.

They placed a hood over her head and tied her hands together. The 'enforcers'—Henrietta Piper Cowan and Christine Smith—set to work. Cowan was seventeen, Smith only sixteen. Ann was punched in the face, so violently that she collapsed to the floor. Blows rained down upon her. She was kicked in the head and belly.

They stopped suddenly. From beyond the door came the sound of a little girl's wailing. Sharlene, missing her mother, had come up the stairs. Elizabeth Douglas had come up behind her, 'Bumper' Graham in tow.

'Get her out of here!' she hissed.

Graham brought Sharlene back down the stairs and out into the street. He gave the child ten pence to 'go buy some sweets for yourself'. When she returned from the shop on the corner he decided it might be better not to have her about the place at all. He bundled her back into the van and drove her to the YWCA hostel. He left her standing on the doorstep and went back the way he'd come, to the place where Ann Ogilby was being savagely beaten.

In the romper room the two teenagers had paused in their brutal battering of the helpless—and at that stage unconscious—Ann Ogilby. They wanted a smoke. Calmly and callously they lit up, laughed and joked, discussed which disco they'd go to that night, until they'd finished their cigarettes.

The punishment was then ratcheted up a notch. Somebody—probably Cowan—began hitting the victim repeatedly with a brick, concentrating on her head. It's probable that those blows hastened Ann's death.

Graham and Joey Brown had come into the room by then. One of them saw the blood staining the sack and realized that the 'punishment' had gone too far. Yet still the two girls continued their frenzied beating.

Finally, after an hour or more, they stopped. Etta Cowan removed the sack. All knew by the sight of Ann Ogilby's disfigured face that she was dead.

The men gathered the body up into another sack and brought it downstairs to Elizabeth Douglas. She evinced no surprise on learning of the murder but instead ordered the corpse to be brought away 'somewhere and dumped'. The teenagers, without any show of remorse or regret, went off to the disco they'd discussed while beating to death the innocent mother of four.

———

In February 1975 eleven women and one man, Albert 'Bumper' Graham, were tried and sentenced for the murder at the Belfast City Commission. All pleaded guilty. The women were arraigned just days before the IRA reinstated its ceasefire, suspended the previous year in the face of Unionist violence. Four days after the sentencing by Justice McGonigal, two Catholic youths were gunned down by the UDA for no reason as they left a church on Malone Road. The slaughter in Ulster was continuing unabated.

Terrorists, especially those operating in the north of Ireland, are often referred to as 'paramilitaries'. I for one have never been comfortable with this term; I feel that it diminishes the standing of the real military. Justice McGonigal appears to have shared this view.

'I do not know what constitutes a "paramilitary" organization,' he said. 'What appears before me today under the name of the UDA is gun law, a vicious and brutalizing organization of persons who take the law into their own hands and who, by kangaroo courts and the infliction of physical brutality, terrorize a neighbourhood through intimidation, and rule an area of this city.'

He sentenced Elizabeth Douglas to ten years in prison for the manslaughter of Ann Ogilby. She received two further sentences of three years each for the crimes of intimidation and for detaining the victim against her will. As is all too often the case, those sentences were to run concurrently with her ten years— presumably the thinking is that the minor crimes were committed *at the same time* as the murder.

She was freed when she'd served half her sentence. Ann Ogilby's four motherless children were taken into care.

MARIE MURRAY, THE ANARCHIST WHO MURDERED A GARDA

Women and armed robbery rarely keep company on this side of the Atlantic. In America it was always otherwise. On 5 February 1974 a sensational news story reached Ireland from Berkeley, California. Patty Hearst, the nineteen-year-old heiress to the Hearst publishing fortune, had been kidnapped by a group of anarchists. They'd given themselves an enigmatic name: the Symbionese Liberation Army. And, as if this wasn't enough drama to be getting on with, more was to follow that coming April. The SLA mounted an armed raid on the Hibernia Bank in San Francisco. There, caught on a closed-circuit TV camera, were the unmistakable features of the kidnap victim. She looked nothing like a victim, however. Dressed in black from head to toe and wielding a Kalashnikov rifle, pretty Patty Hearst was the glamorous apotheosis of the anarchist, a pin-up to rival Cuba's Che Guevara. Armed robbery was sexy again.

In Ireland it was quite another story. There was nothing remotely attractive about the raids the IRA were carrying out on both sides of the border. They were targeting banks, building societies and post offices in a campaign to raise funds for the armed struggle. The government in the South were alarmed. The last thing anybody wanted was for the conflict in the Six Counties to spill over to the republic.

But in February 1975 the Provisionals reinstated their ceasefire and the Irish Government stopped worrying. By this time, though, the republican movement had split and split again, throwing off tiny splinter groups that were getting under the skin of the body politic. They made it known that the PIRA truce did not apply to them, and continued the campaign of armed robbery where the Provos had left off. One such was the Irish Republican Socialist Party.

The IRSP was founded by Séamus Costello, a Marxist committed to the socialist ideal and disenchanted with the way the struggle was progressing in the North. He was vehemently opposed to any appeasement of loyalists and believed that only armed might would win. Marie Murray believed this also. She and her husband Noel joined the movement in 1974.

It was an odd choice for a young woman born and reared so far from conflict. Marie had no firsthand knowledge of being burnt out of her home by rampaging B-Specials, knew nothing of discrimination in the workplace or unjust allocation of housing. She never had to endure taunting and triumphalist marches past her hall-door by men banging drums and carrying curiously atavistic banners. No relative of hers had been interned and tortured without trial, in an eerie foreshadowing of Guantánamo Bay.

This is not to say that Marie knew no personal tragedy. She did, and her early years were cursed by misfortune. She never knew her real parents. She was born in Castlepollard, County Westmeath, which lies some miles to the north of Mullingar, in the shadow of Tullynally Castle. The ancient keep is the ancestral home of the Pakenhams. By a strange quirk of fate one Frank Pakenham was to be the indefatigable defender and friend of another female murderer, the notorious Myra Hindley, when he'd become the fifth Earl of Longford.

Little Marie was put up for adoption soon after her birth. It's believed that her mother was a single girl, forced to give up her baby, as was the practice in 1949. In any event she was adopted by a couple from the area, but lost a mother for a second time when the couple died in a road accident when Marie was eight. She was sent for fostering to County Clare and lived there happily until her late teens.

She was a bright child, excelling at schoolwork and making friends easily. She found herself drawn to the Irish language and enjoyed more than anything else her summer sojourns in the Connemara Gaeltacht. On leaving school she had the opportunity of developing this love of Ireland's heritage: she became a civil servant in Dublin, working within the Department of the Gaeltacht. She left in 1973—at the time the ludicrous rule was still in place whereby a female civil servant must leave should she marry. Her choice of husband, however, was unfortunate: she married Noel Murray.

It was inevitable that the two should meet. Marie's increasing involvement in all things Irish—and in particular all things nationalist—had led her to Sinn Féin, the republican party. In 1973 it languished in a political wilderness; it would be many years before the party would gain acceptance by the mainstream, both north and south of the Border. When Marie came to it, the party was split, each half being the political wing of two rival paramilitary factions, the Official IRA and the Provisionals. Marie sided with Official Sinn Féin.

Her husband to be, Noel Murray, resembled not at all her fellow civil servants, or the gentle people of Clare among whom she'd spent her younger days. He was of slight build, but dark-haired and handsome, a man of action—and a romantic figure for a callow country girl finding her way in the big city. Noel was a native of Celbridge, County Kildare, the youngest son of a farming family. He was skilled with his hands, had learned metalwork when apprenticed at CIÉ, the national transport company, before leaving for a job in Tallaght as a technician. Soon, however, he found himself unemployed. It was at this time that he became involved with the Official IRA. When a further split came in the republican movement he sided with the IRSP, and as part of a small group ran guns and explosives to Northern Ireland. He also robbed banks and the police had a warrant out for his arrest. Noel was, in effect, Clyde Barrow to Marie's Bonnie Parker.

There was nothing romantic, though, about the tragedy that would unfold on 11 September 1975. This personable young woman who'd twice lost a mother had embarked upon a path that would end with her taking the life of a man who, like Marie, held his country in high esteem. He'd sworn an oath to protect and defend its citizens from all harm. His name was Michael Reynolds.

———

Garda Reynolds was thirty-one, a native of Ballinasloe, County Galway. Like Marie Murray, Michael had come to Dublin in the early 1970s. Following his graduation from Templemore he was stationed first in Kilmainham. He was not the only member of his family to choose the Guards: his sister Kathleen was a Bangharda—as the rank was then known—in Pearse Street barracks.

Michael had spent a happy three years at Clontarf Garda station. He liked the locality: situated on the north side of Dublin Bay, it's within easy reach of the centre of town but is at the same time a lovely suburb of well-kept homes lining the road leading to Howth Head. Crime was low in the 1970s: there was only the odd burglary, mugging or act of vandalism. Now and then a gang of youths might steal a car and go joy-riding. Michael was often called on to give chase in a police car, and was therefore no stranger to the high-speed pursuit.

But that day he was out of uniform. He'd been on night duty until 6 am, and had returned home to nearby Artane, where he slept until early afternoon. He'd promised his wife Vera that he'd take her shopping. First, though, he had to collect his pay packet, waiting for him not in Clontarf but in Raheny Garda station. They set off in the family car, their two-year-old daughter Emer safely strapped into the child seat in the back. The drive to Raheny would take no more than five minutes.

In Ballsbridge, across the bay, beyond the twin chimneys of the ESB power station at Ringsend, two young men were stealing a car parked outside the headquarters of the Irish Hospitals Sweepstakes. It was a four-door Ford Cortina—by no means a high-powered vehicle but it would suit their purposes. They needed a car that wouldn't be missed until the close of the working day. The Cortina fitted the bill; they knew it to be a company car and had had it under surveillance from early morning. One of the men wasted no time in picking the lock. He slid into the driver's seat and opened the passenger door. Unremarked on and unnoticed, the two slowly left the carpark and headed for a rendezvous on the north side of the city: St Anne's Park in Clontarf. They'd been there the previous day, putting the final touches to a plan of robbery. They found the ringleader, Noel Murray, in the prearranged spot, in the company of his wife Marie. The two young men had followed their part of the plan in providing the getaway car. The four had earmarked for robbery the Killester branch offices of the Bank of Ireland. It was going to be easy. The Murrays were armed with handguns; the security men at the bank were not.

And crucially—for this particular robbery was to question once again the wisdom of maintaining an unarmed police force when armed robbery was on the increase in Ireland—crucially the Garda Síochána did not carry guns. When the force was established by the young Irish state there were those who felt that Ireland should follow the lead of the United States and other nations and arm the police. After all, the experience of France, Germany and indeed most other countries seemed to suggest that allowing law enforcers to bear arms was a deterrent to serious crime. On the other hand Britain had shown that the alternative worked also. It had been a difficult choice to make but Ireland's founding fathers appeared to have chosen well. Prior to the early 1970s the country seemed set to continue as a relatively firearms-free society.

At about 4 pm the stolen Cortina drew up at the bank. Killester straddles the Howth Road, midway between Clontarf and Artane. Beyond it, to the east, lies Raheny, where off-duty Garda Michael Reynolds had called to pick up his wages. At a little before 4 pm he was westbound again, on his way to the city centre.

Inside the bank the staff and customers were coming to terms with the sudden appearance of two men and a woman. Two carried revolvers and bags made of a sleek brown material. They looked like pillowcases.

'This is a raid!' announced Noel Murray. 'Get back behind the counter.'

The startled staff members obeyed without hesitation. It was clear to all that these were seasoned raiders. On entering the premises they'd fanned out like professionals, blocking the exits and keeping everybody covered. They wore masks. Noel's was a balaclava. He had a Zapata moustache, but that was nothing out of the ordinary in 1975; many young men in Dublin wore one.

Most striking of the three was Marie Murray. For the heist she'd donned an ash-blonde wig that cascaded down past her shoulders. Her face was hidden behind a mask similar to her husband's and, like him and her other male accomplice, she wore a combat jacket. With a revolver clutched in her left hand she was in control, strutting across the bank floor, before clambering over the counter. There were no customers to be seen, only the terrified staff, most of them women.

Marie had rehearsed this until it was second nature; she knew exactly what to do. But she was nervous all the same. She blundered against a weighing scale, sending it to the floor with a clatter. Having ordered a cashier to move aside, she began stuffing her bag with notes.

Meanwhile the third robber had burst into the bank manager's office, surprising him and the bank's sole customer at that hour. She cried out as the masked man levelled his revolver.

'Put your hands up!' he ordered. The manager obeyed. 'And no pressing alarm buttons,' added the raider with menace.

Marie Murray and her gang netted over £7500 in Irish banknotes and twenty-eight American dollars. It was not a great sum but it was hardly more than could be expected from a small local branch. The point was that it was easy pickings. Nobody had got hurt, no member of staff had behaved foolishly and attempted to alert the authorities. As far as the raiders were concerned the Guards would not be in pursuit for some time yet. By the time the alarm was raised they'd be safely on their way, but not in the stolen Cortina; that would soon be abandoned and the gang would go their separate ways.

That's how it should have been. As luck would have it, however, a Guard was already heading their way as they emerged from the bank.

———

Michael Reynolds was approaching Killester shopping centre as the Murrays and their fellow raider were running for the getaway car. Marie stumbled and almost fell in through the rear door as the driver gunned the engine. He hit the accelerator and the car swung onto the road, fishtailing wildly. Michael Reynolds had to swerve to avoid a collision. He turned to Vera.

'I'll bet you any money', he said, 'that that car's stolen.'

'For God's sake, Michael,' she pleaded, 'leave it be. They might have guns.' She was thinking of the Sallins raid of August, carried out by a group of heavily armed men.

Her husband laughed. 'Don't worry,' he said.

He himself wasn't in the least bit concerned. As he floored the accelerator and set out in pursuit he mused that he wasn't doing anything he hadn't done a hundred times before. Still convinced he was dealing with nothing more dangerous than joyriders, he stuck doggedly to the Cortina, sounding his horn continually. Vera said nothing. Little Emer sensed the excitement in the air but didn't cry or call out.

The chase was on. Unknown to Michael Reynolds the bank staff had alerted the Gardaí in Dublin Castle and five squad cars were converging on the area. There was also a civilian involved: Oliver Byrne, a wholesaler from Raheny, had seen the robbery taking place and joined in the pursuit. At high speed the car carrying Marie Murray and her husband roared through Clontarf. Byrne couldn't keep up and fell away, leaving Michael to continue the chase alone.

The getaway car turned into St Anne's Park, closely followed by Michael. As one, the two cars sped along the main avenue. Without warning the Murrays' driver applied the brakes, the car skidded over the grass and came to a halt among the trees. The raiders were out and running along the footpath. They split up into twos.

Michael Reynolds did what his training had conditioned him to do. He gave chase at once on foot, following the woman and her male accomplice. So far he hadn't seen signs of weapons. He was a big man, and very fit. The raiders looked to be out of condition.

'Garda!' he shouted after the fugitives. 'Stop where you are!'

But Vera Reynolds, left behind in the family car with her young daughter, was having grave misgivings. It was four against one and her concern for her husband's safety was mounting. She lost sight of him in seconds as he hurried after the robbers. He'd left the cassette player in the car switched on and there was loud music playing. Vera heard what sounded like the crack of a snare drum. It could equally have been a gunshot from outside. . . .

———

Marie Murray knew it had all gone terribly wrong. She was sweating in her heavy clothing and the long blonde wig as she ran in front of her husband. It had all looked so good and foolproof on paper. 'In and out,' Noel had assured them. 'We'll be out of there before they even know we're robbing them.' He'd planned the escape route down to the last detail: there were no traffic lights. In the unlikely event they were chased, they'd have a clear run.

But where had the big man come from? That's what Marie wanted to know. Noel had cursed all the way to the park, calling it bad luck, and she supposed it was. The pillowcase of money she carried was slowing her down. She thought she heard the wail of police sirens from very close by.

The big man was gaining on them. But Marie was armed: she had Noel's Colt .45 revolver in her jacket pocket, her own in her hand, safety catch off, ready for action.

Now she was running along the bank of a stream. She was panting. She heard Noel urging her on. She wondered if she should jettison the bag of stolen money, let it all go. Her freedom was more important. But how would she explain that to Noel?

The big man had almost closed the distance. And all at once he launched himself into a flying tackle, bringing Noel Murray down. They tumbled down the riverbank in a flurry of limbs.

Marie stopped running. Panic seized her. The big man had Noel in a half nelson and was overpowering him; Noel was fighting back. Unsteadily she aimed the gun, hoping for an opportunity to use it, to disable Noel's attacker, to allow Noel to escape.

'Let go of my fella!' she screamed.

He ignored her, and continued to wrestle with Noel. Marie moved in to stop him, thought she could strike him with her free hand—the one holding not the money but the gun.

The gun went off. The big man slumped to the earth, blood pouring from his temple.

'Aw Jesus, Marie,' was all her husband could say.

They stared at the body on the grass, neither quite believing what had happened. Marie was trembling. Noel took the gun from her. They ran.

——

The first Garda car on the scene was not, as it happened, one of the five that had responded to the alert from Dublin Castle. It belonged to the drugs squad and had been patrolling in nearby Fairview when the call came over the radio. When its three occupants arrived in the park they found a civilian, Raymond Baragy, examining Michael Reynolds. He lay without moving and it was plain that he was seriously injured, probably dying.

'I think his wife is over there beyond,' Baragy said.

Vera was standing by the car when a plainclothes detective approached. She looked concerned but not distraught.

'Where's Mick?' she asked. 'Have you seen Mick? Is he all right?'

The detective didn't know what to say. He knew only that sooner or later the woman would have to identify the man lying beside the stream. He told her what he'd seen.

'Are you a Guard?' she asked.

He nodded.

'So's Mick. Garda Michael Reynolds.'

More police were arriving. Within minutes of the incident all available patrol cars in the area and beyond had converged on St Anne's Park. An ambulance belonging to Dublin Fire Brigade joined them, and its crew rushed Michael Reynolds to Jervis Street Hospital. Within hours he was dead.

The news shocked the police force. It was rare for a Guard to be slain in the line of duty. The decade that had seen so many deaths in the North had known only one other Garda fatality: that of Richard Fallon, murdered in 1970 when he intervened in a robbery on Arran Quay in the city centre. To the men and women—uniformed and plainclothes—massed in St Anne's Park, the shooting of an unarmed Guard was a despicable and cowardly act. They would stop at nothing to find the killer.

They examined the getaway car used by the Murrays. Sure enough the reports that the gang had been wearing disguises were confirmed by the presence of a false beard and moustache. They also found a woman's handbag and hairbrush, but no trace of the loot.

The park was big: all of 260 acres that included football pitches, tennis courts and a pitch-and-putt facility. There were many and ample hiding places for a killer on the run. A helicopter was summoned and tracker-dogs brought in. It was the largest manhunt in many years. But as darkness fell the search had yielded nothing. Garda Reynolds's killers had eluded capture.

———

Marie Murray had discarded the blonde wig and the combat jacket. Dressed now in her green sweater and black trousers she looked as inconspicuous as any young woman emerging from St Anne's Park. She still held the telltale brown pillowcase but had folded it up so that it looked no less suspect than a large handbag. She doubted she'd attract undue attention. She left the park not through a gate but through a gap in a hedge, crossed the road and calmly waited at a bus stop.

A squad car passed by. The occupants did no more than glance at her. She boarded a bus and arrived home in Raheny, to find that Noel had got there before her. The radio was on.

The news, he told her, was not good. She'd shot a member of the Garda Síochána.

Marie listened with mounting dread as the news bulletin spoke of Guard Reynolds's fight for his life in Jervis Street Hospital. Noel made her cups of tea but nothing would quell her anguish. Shortly after 6 pm she heard the grim news: Michael Reynolds was dead.

———

Within days of the killing the trail had gone cold. There'd been sightings of two young men answering the descriptions given of the driver and his accomplice. They'd gone their separate ways, one running across a football pitch in the direction of Raheny, carrying a briefcase. The other had been last seen walking quickly, close to the seafront near the east end of the park. He'd been walking on the grass, even though it was raining heavily at the time.

The manhunt was hampered by the fact that the gang had been heavily disguised. It was impossible to say whether the men had facial hair or were clean-shaven. Gardaí had found parts of disguises in and near the abandoned getaway car, but who was to say that one or more of the fugitives were still disguised when on the run? And no one could provide a satisfactory description of the woman, other than an approximation of her height.

On 12 September, the day after the shooting, the Cabinet met in Leinster House. Later the Minister for Justice announced to the press that a reward was being offered for information leading to the capture of Michael Reynolds's killers: £20,000. It was the largest sum ever offered by the State for information of this kind. If there'd ever been doubt that Irish society stood foursquare behind its police then this offer was enough to dispel it. The clear message was: 'We value our Guards and won't tolerate anybody messing with them.'

Marie Murray was apprehended by a combination of luck and superb detective work. A cleaner working in a public lavatory in Dún Laoghaire discovered a brown-paper bag in one of the cubicles. It contained the two pillowcases, the paraphernalia used in the raid and several Bank of Ireland cash bags—and a single pound note.

The location of the toilets led detectives to believe that the gang were south-siders. Later they would track Marie's journeys on the train shuttle that skirted Dublin Bay and stopped close to Grangemore Estate in Raheny. She'd lived in Dún Laoghaire, knew all the shops there and continued to visit them, even though her current address was on the north side of the city. It made sense: the raiders were locals and were therefore familiar with the layout of the bank; they'd also know when to strike with maximum effect and minimal risk. Sheer ill fortune had placed Garda Reynolds there at the time of the robbery.

Following up a number of leads, the detectives called at the house in early morning. There was nobody home. They picked the lock and waited. At about 8.30 Noel Murray and his wife returned; they'd been walking the dog. The police arrested them without a struggle.

Marie wasn't armed but Noel was. He was found to be carrying two guns. He'd hidden a third weapon under a mattress in a back bedroom. It was the Colt .45 with which Marie had shot Michael Reynolds. There were also bomb detonators and a number of pipe bombs. And money: the loot from the raid, stuffed into two bags the Guards found in a suitcase. Marie and her husband were preparing to leave the country the following week.

When escorted to Ballymun Garda station Marie refused to answer questions, saying that she would talk only to Detective Inspector John Finlay, who was stationed at the time in Donnybrook. He knew the pair. He'd arrested them before for a similar offence. On that occasion Noel had been given a short prison sentence; Marie got off with probation. Now she confessed all to Finlay—apart from the identity of the two accomplices. They were never found.

——

The trial, understandably, was lengthy, extending as it did over seven weeks. In the end both were found guilty of murder in the first degree. Unusually for Ireland in modern times, both were sentenced to death.

So was Marie Murray a cold-blooded murderer? Literally speaking, no. She shot Michael Reynolds when her blood was up, when she and her husband were in desperate circumstances. Though she claimed not to know that Michael was an off-duty Guard, she was very much aware of the approach of his on-duty colleagues: she could hear police sirens approaching the park from many quarters. She feared that her capture was imminent and that she risked a lengthy jail term in Portlaoise Prison. At the time of the shooting only one obstacle stood in her way of escape: Michael Reynolds.

In might be interesting to try to reconstruct those moments. Marie was adamant that she'd never intended firing the gun— that she wanted to use it as a blunt instrument that would disable the man wrestling with her husband. She stuck to her story that the gun went off by accident.

Now, anyone who's ever handled a Colt .45 will know that it bears little resemblance to the diminutive weapon used by Bridget Waters to shoot her husband (see page 84). Fully loaded it weighs a very impressive 2 lbs 13 oz, or 1.27 kilograms. In everyday terms that's the equivalent of carrying more than a litre bottle of water or juice. To fire such a fearsome weapon a woman would have to bring seven pounds of pressure to bear on the trigger—far more than needed to fire an ordinary handgun. It could never have 'gone off accidentally'. Besides, the Smith & Wesson Colt .45 has not one but *two* safety catches. If both are off then you can be reasonably certain that the bearer intends firing the gun.

And so we're confronted with a scenario in which Noel Murray has been wrestled to the ground by a bigger man. At no point is his life in danger; Michael Reynolds means only to restrain him until his colleagues arrive. Nor is Marie in any immediate danger. The Guards haven't even entered St Anne's Park yet. She can't plead a panic situation; there is no immediate risk of her being apprehended. She has several seconds in which to think, to evaluate the situation and to take the most appropriate course of action.

She yells 'Let go of my fella!', moves closer and attempts to strike Michael with the gun. It goes off, as though it's fitted with a hair-trigger.

She could have yelled: 'I have a gun. Let go of my fella or I'll shoot.' She could have fired a warning shot over Michael's head.

Instead she shot him at close range with a heavy-calibre bullet through the temple. It's hard to see her action as being other than deliberate and calculating. And entirely unjustifiable.

Both Marie and her husband stood trial for the capital murder of Michael Reynolds. Each refused to recognize the court, a standard tactic of terrorists, and proceeded to verbally abuse the judge and prosecutors. As a consequence, for much of the seven weeks of their trial the Murrays had to follow the proceedings through loudspeakers in their holding cells beneath the Special Criminal Court, Dublin. In the end both were found guilty and given the most severe sentence known to Irish justice. They were to be hanged on 9 July 1976 and their remains interred in the prison grounds.

The sentence dismayed those who believed that capital punishment belonged to a barbarous past. Yet many welcomed it. 'There was at that time, and I think throughout the seventies,' said the late Éamon Leahy, 'a feeling that where there was an unarmed Garda force in particular, society had to be seen to stand strongly behind them.'

Marie and her husband narrowly escaped hanging. They lost their appeal on 30 July and a new execution date was set. A second appeal on 1 November was successful. The Supreme Court quashed the charge of capital murder and converted Noel's sentence to life imprisonment. Marie gained a retrial and was again found guilty of capital murder. She too served a life sentence.

NORMA COTTER, THE WIFE WITH THE SHOTGUN

The question of alcohol and domestic violence is a vexed one. It becomes even murkier when both husband and wife are heavy drinkers. We're left to wonder if perhaps the woman's drinking might have led to violence in her spouse.

But two American researchers give this theory short shrift. Doctors Glenda Kaufman Kantor and Nancy Asdigian have found little evidence to support the notion that a woman's drunkenness provokes assaults by her husband. They also found that most battered wives 'had not been drinking at the time of the incident of domestic violence'.

It is a fact though, they discovered, that brutalized women 'more commonly report drinking after abuse, suggesting that they drink partly as a way to cope with their physical and emotional pain'.

Kaufman Kantor and Asdigian also learned that many abused women are alcoholics or heavy drinkers because their drinking patterns are similar to their husbands'. In these cases, they conclude, it's 'more likely that the husband's rather than the woman's drinking precipitates the violence'.

Norma Cotter's relationship with her husband would certainly have reinforced the researchers' findings. Aged twenty-six, she was married to Gary Cotter, an army corporal stationed in Portlaoise Prison. He was thirty-eight, a veteran of the Irish army's tour of duty in Lebanon under the aegis of the United Nations.

In late 1994 Portlaoise was the only Irish jail, apart from the Curragh military detention centre, to still have an army presence. The latest IRA ceasefire had been declared that year and there seemed little likelihood that the group would try to spring any of its people housed in Portlaoise. All the same the jail was—and is—heavily fortified both inside and out, capable of withstanding a rocket attack or worse. As part of the army detail, Corporal Cotter would have little or no contact with the prisoners. His duties were to man the perimeter, to be alert at all times. It was tedious rather than high-risk work. Gary couldn't wait for his twice-monthly leave, to go home to Broomfield West, Midleton, County Cork, to do little else but drink, and forget the tedium of his job. He felt he'd earned his whiskey and soda twice over.

The Cotters had an uneasy relationship, and their reliance on alcohol may have been no more than a symptom of a deeper problem. In Norma's words they got on all right: 'not brilliant but you could live with it'—shorthand, most would agree, for an abusive relationship. That both drank to excess was no doubt indicative of a very troubled marriage. Gary had a poor tolerance of whiskey. It altered him, causing him to undergo a personality change. When he drank whiskey he tended to become abusive and beat Norma.

It might not have been so bad had the couple been childless, but they had one child, Christopher, a boy of two and a half. Gary rarely saw him, and certainly never spent time with him. Once home on leave he'd drop the child off at the grandparents' home and Norma and he would go out drinking. Inevitably there'd be a row the following morning about who was going to collect the boy. They usually ended up doing it together. It was as well that Christopher was at Norma's parents' home on 2 January 1995. With two parents who behaved so irresponsibly towards him, his future was going to be bleak enough. He did not need to hear or see what occurred early the following morning.

Some wives might give their husbands golf clubs as Christmas presents. A new dressing gown is also acceptable. Or cuff links, or sports accessories for the car. Instead Norma gave Gary his heart's desire: a double-barrelled shotgun. It was waiting, gift-wrapped and gleaming when he came home on 24 December 1994, looking forward to enjoying a week's respite from Portlaoise. He was delighted. He wondered if she'd thought to buy the proper cartridges to go with it. . . .

With Christopher out of the way, the drinking started. The couple went to the pub shortly before nine on the evening of 2 January. Having had 'one or two' in their local they moved on to a second pub where they met with friends. It was pleasant company.

Norma, however, was keeping an eye on what her husband was drinking. Lager and stout were acceptable; she knew he could handle those. It was the whiskey she feared. It did odd things to him, turned him into a different man entirely. She looked doubtfully at the round bought by their friend Noel Howard. Gary was about to have another whiskey.

'That's an ould black eye for me,' she said. 'Don't give him that.'

But her entreaties fell on deaf ears and by the time they left the pub all had had a considerable amount to drink, Gary more than anybody else. He'd drunk at least eight pints of stout and several whiskeys. Norma had been drinking glasses of cider: five pints in all, perhaps six. They decided to move on to a disco. More alcohol was drunk.

But Gary went home alone. He was tired, he said, and left the club at about 1.20 am. Norma stayed on with her women friends. Later they decided to continue the party elsewhere, were given a lift from the club and stopped off at the Cotters' where Norma collected a bottle of vodka and a flagon of cider before going off again with her friends. It was around 4 am before she finally got home again. By her own admission she was very drunk.

Gary was sleeping when Norma crept into bed beside him. But she was too inebriated to keep quiet and she woke him up. He didn't know what time it was. It was still dark; it might have been evening.

'You better go and collect Christopher,' he said.

'It's too early.'

'Go and collect him anyway.'

'Why me?'

'You're his mother.'

And so it went for twenty minutes or more. Norma was tired too; the drink had made her drowsy. All she wanted to do was sleep. She laid her head on the pillow.

Next Gary knew she'd thrown the covers off and was vomiting over the sheet. He was angry, called her a 'drunken slag', punched her and kicked her out of bed.

Norma's memory of the events of the next few minutes are hazy. She remembers going downstairs once or twice—whether with the intention of leaving to collect her son it's difficult to say. In any case her husband refused to allow her into the bedroom.

She'd had enough. It was time to teach her husband a lesson. She went into one of the spare rooms where she knew Gary had stowed his Christmas present, the shotgun. She wasn't sure how to use it properly. It was new, untried. The firing mechanism looked different from Gary's old gun, a weapon she'd learned to handle well. But he'd removed the firing pin so it was useless. She decided to fetch the new gun. It was in one of the closets, out of their little boy's sight. Gary was still lying on his back in bed with eyes shut, oblivious to her presence in the room.

In a blind rage Norma fired—high, well above the bed, a shot not intended to do any damage at all. The shotgun pellets smashed into a wardrobe. Gary jumped up as though he really had been shot, his army training kicking in. He knew he was in deadly danger.

'I wanted Gary to leave me alone,' Norma remembered. 'I just wanted him to stop coming at me and hitting me. All I wanted to do was go to bed and he wouldn't let me.'

We have Norma's assurance that she didn't mean to fire the second shot. The gun seemed to acquire a life of its own. This is credible. Experts who examined the weapon declared that once the first shot is fired from the one barrel, the recoil will cock the gun for a second shot. This was a hunting piece, designed for clay-pigeon shooting or bringing down live birds. When shooting either, speed is essential. If the hunter should miss the bird with his first shot then he can't waste precious time cocking the gun manually. Norma could hardly have known that her warning shot had primed the shotgun for the second—deadlier—one.

In any case she panicked. The blast would have been deafening in that enclosed space. The force of the recoil would have sent her reeling. It took only a slight pressure on the trigger for the gun to fire the second time.

Gary sat up. In a fraction of a second he assessed the situation. He turned, intending to leap out of bed. That was when the gun discharged itself a second time. The blast caught him in the side and spun him round.

'Oh, Jesus Christ!' he cried. They were his final words. He rolled over on the bed, dead or dying.

Dazed, and still holding the smoking gun, Norma went back down the stairs. She felt frightened. She held onto the gun, afraid that Gary would come after her. She pulled on a coat over her nightdress, went next door to the home of the Dean family and frantically rang their doorbell. It was 5.10 am.

'I'm after shooting Gary,' she told a shocked Ann Dean. 'He kept on nagging me so I went and shot him.'

Mrs Dean phoned the police. When Detective Garda Michael O'Sullivan arrived Norma was drinking black coffee and seemed to be in a more lucid state. He carefully took custody of the shotgun.

At the Garda station she confessed all to O'Sullivan and his colleague Garda Margaret O'Connell. The woman noted that Norma had bruises on her arm. She recollected another incident the previous March when she'd been called out to the Cotter home. There'd been violence involved that time too. Norma had several bruises on her body: on her back, right thigh and right arm. O'Connell asked her about the fresh bruises. Gary had 'pushed' her two nights before. He'd been drunk. They'd both been drunk. In Gary's case Garda O'Connell was seeing a pattern of drunkenness and violence emerging. But Norma Cotter didn't seem to be able to control her drinking either. Hence the shooting.

'If I'd been sober I'd never have done it,' she said. 'I wasn't sober, but I wasn't flaming drunk either. I didn't mean to do it. I just wanted to frighten him.'

———

Norma maintained that she 'just wanted to frighten him'. That's fair enough but most people might argue that it would have been sufficient for her to appear in the bedroom with an unloaded shotgun in her hands. She did not. She went to the trouble of loading it with two No. 6 cartridges. She had to open it, slot one or two cartridges into the breech, close the gun and *take off the safety catch*.

I believe the last is a crucial point. Gary was a soldier and guns to him were a way of life. It seems unlikely that he'd have left a loaded shotgun in a house with a small child, drink or no drink. The army has strict rules governing weapons kept in the home. When not in use a gun should on no account be loaded. Even had he done so then he would never have left the safety catch off—it's second nature for a soldier to put it on when a weapon is stood down, for his own safety as well as for the safety of others.

So Norma had loaded the gun, as she admitted in court. She'd also released the catch. Clearly she meant to fire it. Whether she meant to discharge one barrel or two is all the difference between manslaughter and murder. Did she mean to fire above Gary's head, and then threaten him with the second barrel? She contended that his death was an unfortunate accident and perhaps should have been given the benefit of the doubt. She maintained that had she been sober she'd never have done such a thing: her brain was befuddled by alcohol and she wasn't thinking straight.

But can inebriation be used as a get-out-of-jail card? If that were the case, the drunk driver who kills a child can plead diminished responsibility. On the other hand, a person who drinks to excess in the knowledge that this will impair his judgement is making a conscious choice. He's choosing to relinquish responsibility, to switch off his powers of rational thinking.

This was the dilemma facing the jury who were asked to decide Norma Cotter's culpability when her case came before the courts, in October 1996. Did she mean to or didn't she? The hearing lasted four days and was held in the Central Criminal Court. The six men and six women of the jury deliberated for two hours but failed to reach a verdict. They had to spend the night in a Dublin hotel. The following day they declared a majority decision of ten to two. Norma was guilty of murder. She received a life sentence.

She appealed in 1999, on the grounds that the judge had imposed onus of proof on her. This was wrong, according to the appeal judge. Norma had not been obliged to convince the court that her evidence was true. No picky point of law this, but a matter of justice—a defendant is not obliged to prove her innocence, not in Ireland anyway. For the time being Norma was allowed free on payment of £1000 and an independent surety of another £5000.

A new trial took place in December 2003. The judge, Mr Justice Peart, together with the jury, heard the evidence again—and couldn't but find Norma guilty. She was not a murderer, though; whatever sort of warped relationship they'd had, no matter how often he beat and abused her, she still felt something for her husband. In her right mind she'd never have killed him.

It was manslaughter then, not murder. Before passing sentence, Peart declared that there are 'times when the court's punishment must be tempered with some mercy and compassion'. He gave her three and a half years in jail. The sentence was a formality. The judge decided that Norma had served enough time behind bars and allowed her to walk free.

It was certainly a commendable show of compassion. During her time out on bail, from October 1999 to December 2003,

Norma had met another man and had a daughter by him. Unfortunately she'd been unable to curb her drinking, and her new lover had left her. Now she had two children to rear unaided. She returned to them, picked up the pieces, and today is living a quiet and uneventful life in County Cork.

ANNA MARIA
SACCO AND THE
TEENAGE
ASSASSIN

In the 1990s it was hard to escape the conclusion that Ireland had become a very violent society. This social 'disease' which many had long associated with America's inner cities was here, on our doorstep, and it was very threatening. After dark, there were parts of Dublin city centre considered to be 'no go' areas. The Gardaí acknowledged that the main thoroughfare, the once so fashionable O'Connell Street, was the most dangerous street in Ireland. Muggings, assaults and battery were commonplace.

More frightening still were the random acts of violence committed by young people. We seemed to be witnessing a society that was going out of control. In Tallaght, County Dublin, a boy of fourteen was sitting on a wall outside his home one summer evening in August 1998. He and his young brother were approached by a group of youths who demanded a cigarette. The boy said he had none. For this—and for no other reason, it seems—he was stabbed in the head with a screwdriver. He died a few days later. His killer was sixteen.

There's something very disquieting about a child who kills. More disquieting still is a premeditated act of murder carried out by a minor. When that minor is a girl of fifteen and the weapon is a shotgun then people might shake their heads sadly and say:

'Yes, that's America for you.' But in this case it was not the USA; it was Dublin, and it occurred in 1997, barely seven months prior to the screwdriver slaying.

———

It should have been obvious to Anna Maria that Franco was not the best of marital material. Her family told her so, her friends told her so. The beatings and kickings he administered at the least provocation should have told her so. Often there was no provocation at all. Franco Sacco was a little tyrant, a misogynist and a sadist.

The astonishing aspect of this violence is that it took place *before* the marriage. Yet Anna Maria saw fit to marry him. The couple were wed on her nineteenth birthday, 29 May 1995. They'd been going out together since she was thirteen. Anna Maria had waited a year before plucking up the courage to tell her parents. Understandably, they did not approve. But their objections soon faded because she was 'keeping it in the family', Franco being her father's first cousin. Far more appropriate for Anna Maria to marry one of her own rather than a full-blooded Irishman.

She saw the warning signs—God knows they were obvious enough. She knew in her heart that Franco was a bully and that marriage to him was always going to be a disaster.

Tragically, however, this pretty girl with a sunny personality didn't have much say in her own life. Anna Maria came of an Italian-Irish community. She was born in Ireland and spoke English like a native. Not so her parents. Luigi and Lorna Sacco were elderly, first-generation Italians with a rural background. Their knowledge of their host language was limited to the few words and phrases necessary to serve the customers in their string of chip shops. They did not mix outside their own expatriate community and hadn't learned to integrate, as is the case with many immigrants no longer in the first flush of youth.

Luigi had brought his first cousin to Ireland in 1987, when Franco was eighteen. The lad's prospects in his home-town,

Cassino, had not been good. Luigi Sacco was a prosperous businessman. He trusted Franco, could see in him a hard worker. He may have envisaged the young man taking over the family business sometime in the future. That Franco would almost immediately set his sights on the Saccos' young daughter Anna Maria was not part of the plan.

She did get cold feet though, a week before the wedding. Following a brutal battering she took off for Edinburgh with a friend—a girl, only thirteen at the time, and someone who was to play a most unusual role in the life of Anna Maria and her husband to be. But such were Franco's powers of persuasion, coupled with his fiancée's naïvety, that she returned. The wedding was to go ahead as scheduled.

It was a public secret that Franco was a difficult man to live with. 'He was a hard man,' an intimate of the family said. 'Sometimes he was in a good mood, sometimes in a bad mood.' His bride was to bear the brunt of his bad moods.

The beatings began in earnest shortly after the marriage, Franco determined to impose his will on his wife. So bad did they become that Anna Maria was forced to go to the Gardaí for help. Unfortunately her complaint did little to prevent the violence. (This is no criticism of the authorities; it's notoriously difficult to prove domestic violence unless the culprit is actually caught in the act of physical assault.) In the months that followed, the brutality continued. Again and again Anna Maria would leave home in desperation. But she'd always return. She'd been brought up in Italian society and knew that as a wife 'you make your bed and you lie in it'.

Anna Maria confided in the girl who'd joined her in her flight to Scotland. Let us for the sake of convenience call her Cecilia.

On his marriage to Anna Maria, Franco had taken over the running of one of Luigi Sacco's takeaway restaurants, a chip shop in Rathfarnham village. For this privilege he paid his father-in-law £500 per week. It was a bargain; the shop was a thriving concern. This income, together with a handsome dowry, enabled the poor boy from Cassino to buy a five-bedroomed house in middle-class Coolamber Park, Templeogue. Soon after they moved in, Cecilia came to live with her best friend Anna Maria. She also helped the couple manage the snack bar.

Cecilia was a bit of a tearaway who'd run away from home at an early age. She was not averse to taking drugs of all description: heroin, amphetamines, ecstasy, cannabis, alcohol. She'd been before the courts on a number of occasions for shoplifting and other petty crimes. She would be described as 'very precocious and streetwise for a girl of fifteen'. But she was a loyal friend, as she would soon prove to Anna Maria.

She adored Anna Maria, would go to any lengths for her. Would even kill for her.

———

It's doubtful that Anna Maria should have consciously sought out another man. Her experience with the opposite sex had not given her much cause to trust them. Peter Gifford seemed different, however. He was a barman from Tallaght, and she met him by chance at Club 2000 in the Spawell in late 1995.

It was a brief encounter. A friend of Peter's, a delivery man, had been chatting to three girls in the club, one of whom worked in Luigi's in Rathfarnham. Anna Maria caught Peter's eye and he asked for an introduction. He was clearly interested in Anna Maria because he showed up there the following Wednesday, accompanied by the same delivery man. It was to become a pattern. The two friends and the girls began to see one another at the club every Tuesday night for several months.

It wasn't long before Peter heard about the beatings that Anna Maria was enduring. Nor could he help noticing the physical evidence of the abuse, try though she did to conceal the bruises with make-up, and to arrange her blonde hair strategically across her face. But Peter saw too that she was reluctant to talk about it.

The love affair intensified in the spring of 1996. It was then that she said she was 'fed up' with the beatings and would like to have Franco killed. She came right out with it when they'd had a few drinks. Would Peter, she wondered aloud, be prepared to find somebody to kill Franco for her. He laughed nervously, not for a moment believing she was serious. He made a joke of it, leading her on, promising to find somebody who'd 'take care of it'. The subject didn't come up again for a long while, however, and Peter soon forgot all about Anna Maria's unusual request.

It wouldn't go away, though, because Franco Sacco's reign of terror continued unabated. At the same time, his long-suffering young wife was being thrown more and more into the arms of Peter Gifford. The love affair followed a pattern throughout the summer: Franco would abuse Anna Maria and Peter would be confronted with the damage.

On one occasion she turned up for a date with her arm in a sling; Franco had beaten her with a baseball bat, fracturing a bone. There was a barring order against him, she said. She again asked Peter if he'd got in touch with his friend about the contract killing. The question, not unnaturally, took him by surprise; he'd given the matter no thought whatsoever. Murder and contract killings were entirely alien to him. He told her that the gentleman in question couldn't be reached—he was 'on the run'. She believed him. Despite the injuries and Anna Maria's agitated state, he still refused to take her seriously.

He was not to know that the pretty Italian-Irishwoman did mean what she said, and what she was asking of him. This was the first of three attempts to have someone murder her husband. In desperation she'd given £1000 to a friend of her brother's but he kept the money, did nothing and said nothing.

In the end, Anna Maria's release from her suffering came not from a hitman or a friend of a friend. On the morning of 21 March 1997, Peter was at home, sleeping in after a late shift at the pub, when the urgent ringing of his doorbell woke him. It was Anna Maria. She'd driven to his home with another. Peter saw that the person in the passenger seat was fifteen-year-old Cecilia.

'She's after shooting Franco,' Anna Maria said.

Cecilia was always the loose cannon in the relationship. More than one judge and prosecutor would later declare that she was entirely untrustworthy and an inveterate liar. From what we can gather she seems to have done her best to turn her beloved Anna Maria away from Franco. After each beating Anna Maria would turn to Cecilia for comfort. On one occasion the young teenager told Anna Maria more than she cared to hear. There was more to her husband's perversion than even she had suspected.

'You don't know the half of it,' Cecilia said, and confessed that Franco had been abusing her too.

She claimed that Franco had molested her on numerous occasions, both in the house and in the chip shop, and once had raped her in her bedroom. She couldn't trust him at all. She had to wear a tracksuit in bed.

Worst of all, she said, Franco threatened to kill her if she went to the Gardaí. Anna Maria realized that they had that in common too: she herself had received similar threats. Matters were coming to a head.

A week before Franco's death Anna Maria complained of having candidiasis, or thrush, an infection that made sexual intercourse painful for her. He was not to be put off and demanded what he regarded as his conjugal rights. He struck her on the arm but she still refused. He fetched a belt and began thrashing her. He wrapped the belt around his hand and pressed the buckle against her eye. He used his fists, he kicked her.

She was four months pregnant with their first child but that did not deter him. He threatened to kill her and finally she gave in, painful though it was. Afterwards she went to the bathroom, sobbing and muttering about going to the police. Franco warned her yet again: if she went to the authorities he'd kill her. He told her he didn't care about Irish law. It was different from Italian law and the most he could expect to serve for her death was seven years. No, Anna Maria told him, it was life.

'You know what your problem is?' Franco said. 'You're Irish. You've no Italian blood in you.'

Did Franco expect that an Italian wife would endure his brutality for ever? Perhaps he did. His home-town, Cassino, might be but a short car journey from Rome yet it lies deep in Frosinone, a region not noted for its progressive ways. Women know their place in Frosinone. The code governing the behaviour of girls has resisted change for hundreds of years. You do what your family tell you, no matter how much you suffer. Anna Maria's family knew all about the beatings, that they'd been increasing in intensity—'everybody knew it was going on.'

Later that day Anna Maria went to her mother in Ranelagh. She had her hair down, trying to conceal a black eye. Her mother asked what had happened. Anna Maria fainted and had to be taken to hospital. Here she told of her beatings; the doctors and nurses were horrified.

Yet she returned as always to the house in Coolamber Park and tried to pick up the pieces, to make some sense of the madness. Another blow had been dealt her, this time a cruel, psychological one. Franco had been molesting her best friend. Cecilia had told her more about Franco's abuse of *her*.

It was too much to take. Anna Maria phoned him at the chip shop and confronted him with the accusations. Franco exploded. He wanted to kick Cecilia out of the house, calling her a whore. But he did not and more days passed.

———

Peter Gifford had thought at first that the proposed murder of Franco Sacco was a bad joke. Even when Anna Maria asked him if he'd made any headway with the contract killer, he still regarded it all as the gallows humour of a woman close to despair. On the evening of Wednesday, 19 March 1997, the joke looked set to continue, but at least one of those present in the Sacco takeaway in Rathfarnham village wasn't laughing.

Cecilia was serving in the chip shop together with Anna Maria and her sister Caitriona when Peter Gifford came in, as was his habit when he knew that Franco wouldn't be there. They began to talk about the man who was causing so much grief in Anna Maria's life. She said she'd like to be rid of him.

Peter asked how she thought she could achieve this. By having somebody kill him, she said.

Peter laughed, as did Caitriona. They discussed possible methods of disposal. Someone said they could drown Franco in the bath and cut the body up into little pieces.

'Yeah,' said Cecilia, 'we'll chop him up and stick him in the oven.'

More laughter.

Cecilia suggested they shoot him with his own gun. A good idea, Anna Maria agreed. But who would do it?

'I would,' Cecilia said. Anything to help her best friend.

Peter Gifford laughed again. It was all such good fun. He had some chips and a soft drink, remained chatting for a while, then went on his way.

He was back the following night. Again the three women were serving. Talk turned once more to Franco and what was to be done about him. Again there were jokes made. Peter went off to work at the bar in Tallaght.

At closing time Anna Maria shut the shop and all three women went back to the house in Coolamber Park. Franco was in the sitting-room watching a video of *Heat*. They sat down with him to watch the remainder.

At one point in the film somebody is seen loading a shotgun. All agreed it was similar to Franco's, the one he used for fowling. Cecilia knew he kept it under the stairs. The cartridges used in the film were blue. Cecilia made a remark to the effect that the cartridges Franco used—red in colour—were only for shooting birds and wouldn't kill a person. Franco assured her in no uncertain terms that they certainly would. The film over, Caitriona left for home and Franco retired for the night, leaving Anna Maria and Cecilia watching late-night television.

'Are you coming to bed?' Franco called down in irritation. Anna Maria knew what that meant. Her husband expected sex all the time.

Cecilia had had enough. She said she was going to shoot him. By now Anna Maria was extremely tired—too tired to care whether Cecilia was serious or not.

'Not when he's awake,' she said wearily. 'Later.'

She said goodnight, joined her husband in their bedroom and allowed him to have sex with her. She fell asleep soon after.

In the meantime Cecilia was making her preparations. She went to the storage space under the stairs and took out Franco's gun. She also knew where the cartridges were kept. She loaded the weapon and brought it up to her own room, where she stowed it in readiness under the bed.

She was weary too and fell asleep almost at once. In early morning she awoke to find Anna Maria shaking her roughly.

'Are you going to do it?' she asked. 'Are you going to kill Franco?'

'Yeah,' said Cecilia.

Anna Maria then went down to the kitchen to make coffee. Some moments later she heard a loud bang. Cecilia came rushing down the stairs.

'I'm after killing him!' she cried. 'I'm after killing him.'

Anna Maria couldn't quite believe it. They had joked about it. She'd asked Peter to get somebody to do it. She'd even paid to have it done. But now that it was accomplished the reality seemed unreal. She went upstairs to the bedroom. Cecilia had drawn the curtains but there was enough light to see the prone figure on the bed, the gaping hole where the crown of his head had been, the blood, hair and brain tissue on the headboard and the wall.

She tried to remain composed and told Cecilia to do the same. They went out to her car, calmly stepped in and Anna Maria reversed out of the driveway—almost into the path of a squad car. The Guard in the passenger seat saluted her; he'd bought many a portion of fish and chips in her takeaway. Nervous beyond measure now and trying to appear normal, Anna Maria drove to her mother's restaurant in Ranelagh. She told her what had occurred. Franco was dead. Mrs Sacco's daughter had his death on her conscience.

———

On the morning of 21 March 1997 two young women entered Rathfarnham Garda station in great distress. The younger of the two Garda Ronan Walden recognized 'from her working in Luigi's chipper'. It was Cecilia and she was hysterical. She told him she'd shot Franco Sacco.

At first the Guards thought they were dealing with a hoax or a prank. Girls of fifteen did not blast people with shotguns. But soon the serious demeanour of Cecilia and her companion convinced the policemen that she might be telling the truth. Six Gardaí went to investigate.

They found the lifeless body of Franco Sacco just inside the door of his bedroom in Coolamber Park. It had been wrapped in eight sheets and five bedspreads, two towels and an electric blanket, with only the head and right arm protruding. The bundle resembled a mummy and had been secured with another bed sheet. The 'packaging' had been necessary to absorb the blood that had issued from Franco's body—pints of it, staining the bedclothes and seeping into the mattress. Gardaí found more blood on the walls, along with bone splinters from the skull. A shotgun fired at close quarters can make a terrible mess of a human being.

Sergeant Patrick Normille and another Guard donned gloves, and peeled away the bedclothes and the rest of the 'wrapping'. The en-suite bathroom toilet bowl had shotgun pellets in it, and bloodstains. In the bath there was a basin, a brush and a blood-soaked sponge with what appeared to be human tissue attached to it. Great efforts had been made to clean up all surfaces with blood on them.

They found the shotgun in its own 'slip' or cover, standing in a corner of a utility space under the stairs. Both chambers were empty and the barrel smelled of recently fired gunpowder. They found a number of unused cartridges in one of the other bedrooms. The following day they discovered dozens of boxes of cartridges on the top shelf of the garden shed. Later the Gardaí recovered a cartridge hidden in the chip shop in Rathfarnham. It was found behind the top of the walk-in fridges and the rear wall of the shop. The state pathologist confirmed that it had contained the pellets retrieved from the scene of the crime.

Four days following the shooting Anna Maria made a statement in Sundrive Road Garda station, Rathfarnham. She said that she panicked after the shooting and ran from the house, driving first with Cecilia to Peter Gifford's home. When she told him of the murder he agreed to help them dispose of the body, although he did not, as it turned out.

The upshot of the police investigation was the arrest of both Anna Maria and Cecilia. At first it was unclear which of them—if any—was the guilty party. Anna Maria was charged with unlawful possession of firearms. It was a preliminary to the much more serious charge of murder.

———

By the time the case came before a judge and jury it was clear that Anna Maria had not fired the weapon that had, to paraphrase the words of the prosecution counsel, in essence blown Franco's head off. Cecilia had done it but Anna Maria was behind it.

Peter Charleton sc told the court that there had been 'disharmony' in the Sacco marriage and 'unhappy differences' between Franco and Anna Maria. Presumably he meant that the differences between them were those of violent predator and docile prey.

Nevertheless the law demanded that Anna Maria be proved guilty beyond all reasonable doubt of the slaying of her husband, or else acquitted. That was going to be difficult. Charleton's contention, on behalf of the prosecution, was that she'd handed the shotgun to Cecilia with instructions to go upstairs and shoot Franco. But the only evidence to support this was that of Cecilia, who had admitted to the murder. The jury couldn't agree on a verdict and Anna Maria was remanded on bail.

Cecilia was sentenced to seven years in prison but allowed out on probation. She was in more ways than one a problem child. The court of appeal, presided over by three judges, admitted that the state had no provision to detain her. In other words she was too young to be sent to an adult jail.

In the end Cecilia's appeal was heard for the second time in November 1999. It was decided that she was behaving herself, that her probation was proving a success. She'd settled down to a normal life, working as a trainee hairdresser. She was once again living with her parents and they were keeping an eye on her now, ensuring that she honoured the terms of her probation.

With Franco two years dead, there was no more threat to Anna Maria Sacco's health and well-being. Cecilia could hang up her guns. She was no longer a danger to society. The Gardaí would still keep tabs on her and her case might be reopened at any time. For now she was free to go, and get on with her life.

And Anna Maria herself? Some months before, in March 1999, her case was heard for the second time. Fifteen days into the trial, the jury found that there was no evidence to show that she'd done or said anything to encourage Cecilia to shoot her husband. Oddly enough this evidence hinged on Cecilia's accusations of sexual abuse against her by Franco. The judge made clear that those had been a tissue of lies. The girl was therefore a most unreliable witness. Anything she'd said that would implicate Ms Sacco in her husband's murder was to be ignored.

The jury duly complied. Anna Maria walked from the court a free woman. She was carrying in her arms her three-year-old daughter, conceived a few months before Franco Sacco died.

KAREN McDONNELL AND THE DEATH OF A SECRET SOLDIER

'Who'd do this to Joe?' Karen McDonnell wailed. Nobody in the park knows he's a soldier. Who'd want to kill him?'

It was Sunday, 8 June 1997, and the soldier lay dying on his living-room floor, the result of a deep gash in his chest. The 'park' she referred to was McNeill Park in Moorfields, a leafy, middle-class suburb lying hard by the town of Ballymena, County Antrim. The largely Protestant locality is noteworthy for being the birthplace of a Hollywood star and a turbulent priest, respectively Liam Neeson and Ian Paisley Sr.

Joe McDonnell, however, had always been careful of his privacy. In 1997 Ulster was at peace with itself and had returned to a state of relative normality—in so far as the Six Counties could ever be a normal society. The IRA ceasefire of 1994 was still in place and there were moves afoot to set up a new power-sharing executive; the Good Friday agreement was tantalizingly close.

But Joe was a soldier, and no ordinary one at that. He was a corporal in the Royal Irish Regiment, arguably the most hated branch of the British Army serving in the North. To understand the republican and nationalist hatred it's useful to consider how the regiment came about.

When the state officially known as Northern Ireland came into being in 1921 it was felt that it needed a police force that would be quite unlike the British model. The IRA were as active as they'd be for many decades and so the police would of necessity be armed. The Royal Ulster Constabulary (RUC) was set up in 1922, and many of its members were drawn from the old Royal Irish Constabulary (RIC). But from the outset the police force was predominantly Protestant—and still is to this day.

Within the RUC was a special paramilitary force: the Ulster Special Constabulary (USC). The abbreviation will no doubt be unknown to most readers but few will fail to recognize the name by which this force-within-a-force came to be called in the parlance of the people: the B-Specials. If the RUC was made up of a smattering of Catholics then the B-Specials were wholly Protestant. Throughout the following decades they were to acquire the reputation of being the most sectarian force in Europe, feared by nationalists and known to demonstrate their bigotry in violent ways. Such was their shameful record that in April 1972 the British government disbanded them and replaced the force with the UDR, the Ulster Defence Regiment. It was unfortunate that its abbreviation UDR was so close to UDA, thereby linking it in the minds of the nationalists in the North with the terror organization the Ulster Defence Association. There are many who see little difference between the two.

It will be noticed too that, by this act, a body of civic police became a true military force, although the UDR were regarded more as a militia. They proved to be just as sectarian and vicious as their predecessors and were responsible for many outrages, not least being the murder of three members of the Miami Showband in July 1975.

The UDR amalgamated in 1992 with the Royal Irish Rangers, to become the Royal Irish Regiment (RIR). It was thought that a name change might give the regiment more cachet and go some way towards ridding it of its less than illustrious reputation. To nationalists it was of course no more than a cosmetic exercise—it was bigotry under another name, business as usual.

A member of the security forces in Ulster lived on a knife-edge of danger. Almost one thousand had been killed since the Troubles began in 1969. Of this total more than two hundred were serving with the RIR or its predecessor. They were a favourite target of snipers and other would-be assassins.

It was therefore crucial as a serving RIR-man to keep your private life secret. Once out of uniform your occupation was known only to friends, relatives and a trusted few. Thus it was with Joe McDonnell. He was forty-one, with a number of years still to go before retirement. In 1997 life seemed to be on an even keel again. He'd go off to the barracks in the morning, don his uniform there, put in a day's work either on light patrol or training, and come home in the evening to his thirty-two-year-old wife Karen.

———

The call was logged by the Ballymena RUC at about 10 pm on 8 June. A woman was on the phone and she sounded hysterical. It was hard to follow her words; they were garbled and incoherent. She could have been drunk, but one thing was clear: a man had been stabbed. It was an emergency.

Detective Sergeant Michael Braithwaite and a colleague sped to the McNeill Park address. They found Joe McDonnell lying on the kitchen floor, blood pouring from his chest, just under the collar bone. He was still barely conscious, groaning and moving feebly.

'Where's the ambulance?' Karen shouted. 'I thought you were the ambulance.'

It was obvious that she was drunk. At that moment the back door to the kitchen opened and a neighbour, Linda McCrystal, came in. She'd seen the police car with flashing light and come to investigate.

'What happened?' Braithwaite asked as the other constable examined the wounded man.

'I didn't stab him!' Karen blurted out.

'No one's saying you did, madam,' Braithwaite said. He turned to Linda McCrystal. 'Could you phone an ambulance?'

While the call was being made the officers tried to do their best for Joe, raising him into a recovery position. But he was unconscious now and losing blood fast. Karen was wild-eyed. There was a heavy smell of alcohol in the kitchen. There was also a kitchen knife lying next to the wounded man; it was slick with blood. Braithwaite's colleague bagged it for later tests.

The ambulance arrived with siren wailing and Joe was bundled into it. Karen wanted to go with him, but the sergeant wouldn't allow it. He had some questions to put to her. Mrs McCrystal left with reluctance.

Calmer now, Karen accepted a cigarette and made herself comfortable in the living-room. Braithwaite wanted to know where she'd been at the time of the stabbing.

'I was upstairs,' she told him. 'Someone must have come in and stabbed him. I was in bed when I heard him shouting and ran down and saw him there.'

She leaned forward to stub out her cigarette. It was then that the sergeant noticed a large bruise on her shoulder. It was hard to say how recent it was.

'Did you and your husband have a row?' he asked.

She nodded. 'We had a row every day. He threw me down the stairs.'

———

Joe McDonnell was in very bad shape on reaching the Antrim Area hospital. The wound in his chest was five inches deep; the knife had pierced a lung. He was bleeding both internally and externally. A team of surgeons fought to save him but he died of cardiac arrest without recovering consciousness. There was no one to identify his mysterious assailant.

'Nobody in the park knows he's a soldier,' Karen had said. But the RUC did not for a moment entertain the notion that the stabbing was the work of republicans, or even a case of somebody carrying out a revenge attack. This was no assassination.

The knife had been wielded by somebody facing the victim. It had struck down at an angle, piercing the chest between the second and third ribs. There was also evidence that Joe had been drinking heavily: he was more than three times over the legal limit for driving. He could have drunk up to eight pints of lager or twelve shorts.

There were only two people in the house that evening; there'd been no sign of a break-in. The RUC concluded that Karen might have a little more explaining to do. They brought her in for questioning.

Bit by bit they were piecing together the reality of the McDonnells' marriage. The picture that emerged was not pretty. Karen was a divorcée, and an alcoholic. Her drinking had caused her first marriage to disintegrate, losing her the custody of two teenage sons.

She'd married another heavy drinker, Joe McDonnell, and the marriage was a succession of drunken binges accompanied by blazing rows. They were fighting every day it seemed.

Braithwaite cautioned her. He had to repeat the caution because Karen was still very drunk. She'd calmed down considerably, however, and was ready to answer questions. She changed her story. There was no mysterious assailant; she herself had stabbed Joe. The sergeant arrested her.

At her trial in April 1998 in Ballymena it emerged that Karen had been trying to do away with Joe for some time. Some months before the stabbing she'd approached a loyalist who'd been convicted and served time for the illegal possession of firearms. She'd offered him £1000 to kill her husband. On hearing this, a murmur of astonishment passed among the jury of four women and eight men. It was a derisory sum for a man's life. It goes without saying that her offer was turned down.

She approached somebody else and the prosecutor had him testify. It emerged that he was having an affair with Karen. She confided to him that she'd only married Joe for the financial security he could give her. She didn't love him at all and she asked the friend his advice on the best way of 'getting rid of him'.

Karen claimed that the stabbing was accidental but the evidence was against her: the angle was one an assailant would use when intending to kill or injure. The pathologist's report stated that only a slight degree of force would have been needed to inflict the wound. Moreover, Joe would have to have been doubled over and running forward were he to have 'accidentally' run into the knife.

The court heard how Karen and Joe had been having their usual heated, alcohol-fuelled argument. A few days earlier he'd thrown her down the stairs; that accounted for the bruising. From then on she'd slept in a back bedroom.

On the night of the killing, she said, it was Joe who lifted the knife out of the kitchen block and came at her with it. He nicked her but she managed to dodge a second attack. She reached for a second knife.

'He went to go for me again,' she said, 'and I had the knife in my hand. It just went into him and he fell back. I didn't deliberately stab him.'

The prosecutor, Gordon Kerr QC, insisted that it was either an accident or murder, not self-defence: the angle of the stab-wound ruled out the last. She'd lied to her neighbours, blaming the attack on an old boyfriend, then changed her story again, explaining that she was 'confused' when drunk.

He made a big show of Karen's drinking. Joe was the one who'd persevered with all her binges, he contended, saving her from herself and demonstrating his love for her. But she kept going back to her drinking, showing that she cared nothing for him.

'You might think there's an element of despising the man who was prepared to take her back time after time,' Kerr told the jury, 'to go looking for her and rescue her from her drinking.'

He was glossing over the fact that Joe died with enough alcohol inside him to addle a donkey. But the jury members had probably made up their minds by then. It took them a little over an hour to return with a unanimous verdict of guilty. Justice McCollum

handed down the mandatory sentence for murder: life imprisonment for a minimum of twelve years.

On hearing this, some of Joe's relatives raised a chorus of 'Yes!'
while others wept with relief. Afterwards his mother made a short
statement to the press.

'Justice has been done,' she said. 'It won't bring back my son but
at least we know that justice has been done. I'm feeling relieved.
This is the verdict we wanted.'

———

This story has a bizarre sequel. In 1999, having spent a year in
Maghaberry Prison, County Antrim, Karen married a fellow
inmate. The nuptials sent shockwaves of disgust through
Northern Ireland, affecting in particular relatives and friends of
the bridegroom's victim. John Murdock was serving time for the
gruesome killing of his partner.

The former Northern Bank assistant manager strangled Norma
in their home following a row. Though they'd been together for
ten years Murdock had been having an affair with another.
Norma found out. Having killed her, he drove her body to a
remote spot and set the car alight. He went to work the following
day as though nothing had happened. He'd intended reporting
her as missing but the police got there before him. He hadn't been
thorough enough with the burning of the car.

The odd couple—the knife-wielder and the strangler—were
permitted to see each other but once a month. They applied to be
allocated more time together but were unsuccessful.

John Murdock regained his freedom in 2003, having served out
his ten-year sentence. In June 2004 his wife appealed for early
release so that they could be together. Karen claimed that adverse
media coverage of her new marriage had 'demonized' her. The
appeal judge, Sir Brian Kerr, assured her that it was the gravity of
her crime that precluded leniency. Still behind bars, she will not
even be considered for release before 2009.

LORRAINE FARRELL: THE DRUGS BARON AND THE DOUBLE PLOT

He was one of Ireland's wealthiest men, with a personal fortune estimated at forty million Irish pounds, the equivalent in 1996 of eighty million euro in today's money. You wouldn't have found his name on the membership list of the K-Club, though, or seen his smiling face in the society glossies. For Paddy Farrell's millions were drug profits.

He was buried on Sunday, 15 September 1997 in Cloughoge cemetery in a plot that overlooks the city of Newry, with the Dublin Road to the left and a British Army watchtower not two hundred yards away, beyond the railway viaduct. Had his dead girlfriend had her way, they'd have been interred together as lovers sometimes are, in particular those who die as a result of a suicide pact. But there was no pact, only the suicide of one of the lovers. Paddy Farrell, at forty-nine, had no intention of shuffling off the mortal coil for some time to come. He'd already thwarted a number of attempts on his life, all made by the worst desperadoes north and south of the border. Perhaps the last person on earth he suspected of plotting his murder was his own lover, Lorraine.

By most standards it was an unusual relationship. Take the surname for starters. He was Paddy Farrell, she was Lorraine Farrell. He lived in a small mansion off the Dublin Road with his wife Ann and their three children. Paddy and Lorraine came from two unrelated branches of the Farrell clan. She, a pretty and outgoing twenty-nine-year-old, was deeply religious and God-fearing; he was a drugs baron who'd established an empire through racketeering and violence.

They met in Newry when Lorraine got a job there. Soon they were spending a great deal of time together. Their love-nest was in Drogheda, in a small two-up, two-down house belonging to Lorraine's mother. It was in Boyle O'Reilly Terrace, close to Our Lady of Lourdes Hospital. Her mother, Peggy Farrell, shared the house with her live-in partner, Dessie Wilton; together they operated a taxi-hire firm in the town.

Lorraine returned home to Drogheda in 1996, with news that she had a new boyfriend, a well-to-do man from Newry. He came to call on her, with growing frequency, and was in the habit of staying over, sharing her bedroom on occasion. Paddy Farrell's visits became the talk of the little street. Not that the neighbours knew who he was; it was his car that caused the curtains to twitch. The like of Paddy's top-of-the-line maroon Mercedes had never been seen in the terrace. He was 'a successful businessman', the neighbours were told, born and raised in the townland of Annaghgad, near Cullaville, South Armagh. He owned car dealerships and other import/export businesses, he played the stockmarket and had the reputation of being a wise and prudent investor.

All this was true. Though it might have come as a shock to the good people of the street had they known at that time the extent and nature of Paddy Farrell's *real* business.

His empire had three principal enterprises: money laundering, illegal banking, and drug smuggling. It will never be known for certain which branch was the most successful but the trade in illegal substances was the one for which he was known best. It was a mark of his cleverness that he never became directly involved in drug trafficking but was the brains behind the operation.

He came to the attention of the authorities in 1994 when an unusually large shipment of cannabis was intercepted at the port of Rosslare. It proved to be one of many such consignments that were part of a web of smuggling involving at least four European countries.

At the Newry end was Paddy Farrell, ready to convert the drug money into laundered banknotes. This he achieved using as a base a series of bureaux de change near the border. It would be 1999 before the ring was infiltrated and many of the foot-soldiers and ringleaders rounded up.

However, it took two and half years for the investigators to wind up the operation. A year before Paddy Farrell's death the Criminal Assets Bureau began looking into the huge amounts of cash passing between the Republic and the Six Counties. The drug money, and profits made from the illegal sale of tobacco, were being converted into sterling; later into sterling drafts. The last would be ploughed back into the illegal activities.

In 2002 the authorities realized how big the smuggling operation had become when police in Belgium seized a lorry transporting a shipment bound for Ireland. The haul of drugs was estimated to have a street value of €30m. It consisted of more than one million ecstasy tablets, thirty-four kilos of heroin, and hundreds of kilos of amphetamines and cannabis. Who precisely was behind the shipment remained a mystery. What is certain is that the individual—or individuals—involved had filled the breach left by Paddy Farrell.

There were many contenders to take his place as the biggest drug lord of the border areas. Many of those who tried died as violently as he did. In their cases, though, it was the Provisional IRA who ended their careers. The republican group was never happy with the gangsterism that grew in the wake of the violence in Northern Ireland. The drug traffickers gave the IRA a bad name. Drugs were synonymous with the loyalist terror groups; it was felt that republicans should not get their hands dirty in the same way.

One young man had come to their attention: Brendan 'Speedy' Fegan, a lieutenant of Paddy Farrell. He played a risky game, having links to the drugs gang that murdered the journalist Veronica Guerin while at the same time working as a police informant. They called him Speedy because he enjoyed life in the fast lane, whether racing ponies and traps on the A2 between

Newry and Warrenpoint, or driving fast, expensive cars, the fruits of his drug dealing.

He led a dangerous life and took tremendous risks. At one time he was buying drugs in Dublin and selling them on to the UDA in Belfast. He and Paddy Farrell parted company in August 1997, when he double-crossed his boss on a large consignment of cannabis. He needed the money. Whereas Farrell invested his earnings wisely, Speedy was a spendthrift, blowing the profits on cars, women and gambling almost as soon as he made them.

The IRA would end his career in May 1999, in a pub in his home-town, Newry, on a Sunday afternoon. Two gunmen put fifteen bullets into his head. He was twenty-four.

He was the tenth drug dealer assassinated by the group since it went on ceasefire in 1994. But they never came after Paddy Farrell. He was too valuable to them. If a 'volunteer' on the run needed a safe house to hole up in, Paddy was the man to provide it. If you needed money laundered for the 'cause', Paddy was your man. They left him alone to continue his business, provided he didn't cross them.

When news emerged of Paddy's death there were many who drew the immediate conclusion that the drug baron had somehow used up his credit with the IRA. Either that, or a rival gangster had sent a hit team to remove him. It seemed incredible that the man who held so much power in the border counties could die in such unexpected circumstances.

———

Lorraine Farrell's cardinal error was to think that Paddy loved her in the same way as she loved him. It never seemed to occur to her that she was no more than a plaything to him. He never spent even a small fraction of his ill-gotten millions on her, never brought her with him on trips abroad, never gave her expensive presents. Never, in short, did he treat Lorraine the way a rich man is supposed to treat his mistress.

When they met it was in secret and in out-of-way places. To be fair to Paddy, for him to be seen with her in public places might have attracted the unwelcome attention of the authorities or rivals. Nevertheless it must have occurred to him that a romantic evening should have been more than a tryst in her bedroom in her mother's little house in Drogheda whenever the mood took him.

The truth he withheld from Lorraine was that he cared nothing for her. In fact he cared little for the women in his life. Lorraine would have been shocked to learn that she was only one of many girlfriends. She knew he had a wife and children in Newry—he talked about them often—but knew nothing of his past, knew nothing about the women he'd lived with when in Britain too, one of whom had borne two of his children.

At the beginning of September Paddy dropped his bombshell. He was leaving the country. Ireland had become too 'hot' for him. There were too many people who wished to see him, if not dead, then moved to one side. The police on both sides of the border were closing in too, following yet another seizure of drugs bound for the North. They'd been left in a hotel near the border—a drop. Both the RUC and the Garda held the drop under surveillance but nobody showed. Paddy was too cunning for that. They still couldn't trace the massive drugs operation to him, but they were getting closer by the day.

'I'm retiring,' he told Lorraine. 'I'm getting out. We're going to Florida.'

She'd brightened at this, believing that he was asking her to accompany him. She was mistaken. It was his way of breaking up with her. When he left it would be with his loving wife and children.

Something died inside Lorraine that day. A friend who knew her well reported that she went 'off the rails', began behaving strangely. No wonder. This man had been her life. He'd meant everything to her, and it broke her heart to discover that she'd meant so little to him.

Well, she thought, if I can't have him then nobody else will.

She knew somebody who owned a shotgun, a legally held weapon he used for hunting. She'd heard he was looking for a buyer for it. Lorraine expressed interest. But, she explained, she'd need to borrow it first for a couple of days. Get the feel of it. It might not suit her, and it was expensive. The friend agreed readily.

The following day she did a very odd thing. She went to an undertaker's. It was only a few doors away, at number twenty, and owned by neighbour and family friend Patrick Townley. She enquired about a plot in her local cemetery. It was to be a double plot, a 'his and hers' plot, she joked. Townley considered it an odd thing for a young woman to ask but nevertheless accompanied her to the cemetery. With the help of a gravedigger Lorraine chose a site close to where her grandmother was buried. Having returned to the undertaker's she made enquiries about the cost of embalming, much to Townley's surprise. The price he quoted was too high for her; she settled for the time being for the plot. She paid him £200.

On the morning of Wednesday, 10 September, Paddy drove to the little terraced house in Drogheda and parked his car in the usual place. He rang the bell and Lorraine admitted him. She was alone, as he'd expected. Both her mother and Dessie Wilton were at work.

As usual, Paddy wasted no time. He'd come for sex and wanted it right away. Lorraine brought him up to her room as she'd always done.

One wonders if their last bout of lovemaking was as passionate as all the others had been. Did Lorraine enjoy it more because she knew it would be their last? Or did she fake a passion she no longer felt when in the arms of the man who had betrayed her?

Paddy probably enjoyed his last fling with Lorraine. She might even have attempted to tire him out, to have him make love so energetically that he'd fall asleep as soon as they were done. That would have suited her purpose. Or he might have agreed instead to a little sex game. They may have played it every time he visited; they may have jokingly called it Blind Man in the Buff. We can but conjecture. What we know for certain is that when Paddy Farrell died he was naked and blindfolded.

Lorraine's lover would have trusted her implicitly, knowing

that she was malleable. He would surely not have been on his guard in the only 'safe' house he knew, even though he was a man accustomed to danger and the first smell of it.

She was taking a tremendous risk all the same. He might have heard her reach under the bed and bring out the loaded shotgun. But she would have made sure that the safety catch was already off and the gun was ready for use—the friend she'd borrowed it from had given her a brisk demonstration of how those things were done. She went as close as she dared and gave Paddy both barrels.

He died instantly with half his head blown away. Nothing could have prepared Lorraine for the deafening noise of the blast in that small room, or for the amount of blood and tissue that spurted in all directions, even onto herself. She must have made more than one attempt to eject the spent cartridges from the gun. It must have taken all her courage to reach under the bed again and fetch the other two, load them into the breech and aim the gun for a second time.

Like Paddy, she would have felt no pain when the double blast removed the back of her head. The force of the explosion flung her back against the wall. She slumped to her knees, dead, the gun at her feet.

No one heard Paddy's mobile phone ringing a few minutes later.

Dessie Wilton and Peggy Farrell, Lorraine's mother, left work as usual at 5.30 pm and returned to Boyle O'Reilly Terrace. They noticed that Paddy Farrell's big Mercedes was parked in the street. It was hard to miss. They let themselves in and Peggy put on the kettle for tea.

There was no sound from upstairs but Peggy wasn't one to pry anyway. Before Dessie switched on the television he thought he heard a mobile phone ringing and ringing. He decided that Lorraine and her lover were asleep. Peggy and he settled down to watch the football on the telly. Paul Gascoigne was playing for England and was tipped for great things. Moldova hadn't a chance.

Just before the half-time whistle blew, David Beckham took a corner kick. The Moldovan goalie managed to punch it out of harm's way, but once again Beckham took possession. He crossed to Paul Scholes. Dessie Wilton jumped to his feet in excitement as Scholes headed the ball into the back of the net. A phone rang again upstairs. Then another. Two mobile phones ringing and nobody answering either of them.

'Are those two in or what?' Dessie said.

'Well, the car's outside,' said Peggy, 'so I imagine they must be.'

Dessie was growing concerned. The two telephones started up again. Something was wrong. He went up the stairs, calling out Lorraine's name as he went. He knocked on the door. One of the mobile phones rang again. He opened the door. The room was in semi-darkness. In the half-light he could make out the figure of Paddy Farrell sprawled on the bed. Dessie was immediately embarrassed. He didn't want to disturb a sleeping man. He wondered where Lorraine had got to.

When he came downstairs again the match had heated up. Forty seconds into the second period Wright scored from the penalty area with a superb goal that Gascoigne had set up for him. England were leading 2-0. It was Gazza who took the third goal and Wright the final one. Dessie was jubilant.

A phone rang once more upstairs. Dessie went and called out to Paddy Farrell. There was no reply.

When he came back down again he found Peggy with her daughter's handbag on her lap. She was holding a note and shaking. It was from Lorraine, written to her sister Wendy. It was a suicide note.

Dessie raced upstairs for the third time. He threw open the door and switched on the light.

The first thing he saw was the blood. It seemed to him as though a bag filled with the stuff had exploded in the middle of the room, drenching everything. Paddy Farrell lay sprawled on the bed, naked. At first Dessie thought he was wearing a red cap but saw then that it was the blood-soaked blindfold.

He turned away in fright—and nearly tripped over Lorraine's corpse, just inside the door. She was still crouched where she'd slumped down, the gun lying in a dark pool of her partly congealed blood.

Dessie ran to a neighbour a few doors down the street: Patrick Townley, the undertaker, the man who'd sold Lorraine the plot. In his shocked state Dessie had thought it best to summon an expert on death. A doctor would have been no help anyway: Townley discovered that *rigor mortis* had already set in. The couple had been dead for many hours.

There could be little doubt about Lorraine's suicide. Though many thought at first that the double shooting might be a cunningly rigged underworld assassination, the note she'd written to her sister was genuine. Heartbroken at Paddy's betrayal, Lorraine saw no other course but to kill him first and then herself. It was the action of a terribly distraught woman.

She could not have been in her right mind either when buying the double plot in Drogheda. Had she given it coherent thought, she'd have concluded that Paddy Farrell's next of kin would never have countenanced him being buried next to his lover. There was consequently no Romeo and Juliet ending to the affair. Lorraine shared the plot with no one when they interred her there the day after Paddy's remains were being removed from St Catherine's Church, Dominic Street, Newry.

There was much media presence at his burial. The death of a drugs baron always excites great interest. His family and close friends, though, were adamant that Paddy Farrell was nothing of the sort. One man insisted that the deceased was actually a very religious family man, who gave freely to charity. He could not, however, account for the presence of so many beefy bodyguards at the funeral.

As is so often the case when the head of a criminal ring dies, the illegal activities he was accused of did not abate. The vacuum he left was always going to be filled. It was a question only of who was going to fill it, and there were many pretenders to the throne. Before long it was business as usual in the murky world of drug trafficking. Lorraine Farrell's taking of Paddy's life and her own had made such little odds.

JULIE McGINLEY AND THE SHALLOW GRAVE IN LEITRIM

No living person can say with certainty when Julie McGinley went from being a Fermanagh housewife to a sex slave. At the time of her husband's death the pair were operating a blackmail racket. Julie would have sex with men in hotel rooms and Gerry would photograph them in compromising positions. He would then demand money on threat of handing over the incriminating evidence to spouse or employer. It worked well: with the proceeds Gerry was able to build a large house with its own extensive grounds in Ballinamallard, a village to the north of Enniskillen.

It was August 2000. Julie was twenty-eight, a very attractive honey-blonde; Gerry was a handsome thirty-three, a native of Manorhamilton, County Leitrim. They had two young daughters, ages six and four. To the casual observer there was little out of the ordinary about Gerry. He seemed not unlike any other hard-working businessman. He owned a furniture shop in Enniskillen, and did a brisk enough trade. No one thought to question how it was that this modest business could support the couple's free-spending lifestyle.

Blackmail is always a dangerous game. It can rebound on the perpetrator if he isn't very careful in his choice of victims—or if his greed leads him to milk his victim so dry that the victim takes desperate measures. Gerry McGinley must surely have known the risks. He chose to either ignore them or weigh them against his illicit earnings. When he disappeared on Sunday, 13 August 2000, there must have been rejoicing from many quarters in Enniskillen and beyond.

He left without a trace. He'd been last seen the previous evening. Julie and he were enjoying their customary Saturday night drink in the Fort Lodge Hotel. They were in the company of Gerry's business partner Michael Monaghan, and Patrick McPadden, a close friend from Leitrim. Those who saw the four laughing and chatting reported nothing out of the ordinary. Julie had her standard two drinks and no more; she was driving.

As usual it was quite late when the couple returned to their home in Ballinamallard: about 2.30 am, according to their babysitter, Heather Edwards. The girl thought nothing of the fact that Julie came in alone, muttering something about Gerry McGinley being 'out the back'. Sure enough, Heather remembered seeing a man wearing a white tee-shirt coming round the side of the house and going indoors just as she was leaving with Mrs McGinley. He had Mr McGinley's build— athletic—and the same dark hair. She felt sure, however, that Mr McGinley had left earlier that evening wearing a blue shirt, not a white tee-shirt. But she caught only a glimpse of the man before he disappeared. And she'd no reason to suspect that all was not kosher.

Heather Edwards returned with her sister the following morning. Though she saw no sign of Gerry McGinley, she did see his wife and the children. She could not fail to notice too that two men were standing chatting at the back of the house, beside Gerry's white van. Again she'd no reason to suspect that something might be wrong.

But that day nobody saw Gerry. Nor was there any sign of him the day after. The children were asking questions: Where was Daddy? Julie confessed that she didn't know. But it was all right, there was nothing to get alarmed about. Daddy sometimes went off on business. And he always came back, didn't he?

On the third day following his disappearance, however, Gerry's wife could no longer keep up the pretence that all was well. People were on the phone continually, customers from the furniture shop, creditors. Where was he?

On the fourth day there was still no sign. Julie and the children had to face the possibility that Gerry McGinley might not be coming back at all. Heather Edwards stopped by again. This time she mentioned having seen the man in the white tee-shirt, and wondered if there was something wrong. Julie's response was very odd indeed.

'You're very observant, Heather,' she said. 'Maybe you should be looking for a solicitor.'

The babysitter didn't know what to make of it. The whole affair was very puzzling.

By rights Julie should have gone to the police. She did not; somebody else did that for her. It was a neighbour, Robert Elliot. He and Gerry were very close and hardly a day passed without the one looking in on the other. Unknown to Julie her husband had arranged to see Elliot about a business matter on the afternoon of Monday, 14 August. Gerry hadn't phoned to explain, hadn't called along in person. Elliot's suspicions were aroused and the RUC called in. They paid Julie a visit.

The story she told did not quite chime with that of the babysitter. According to Julie her husband had been extremely depressed during the weeks leading up to his disappearance. She was greatly concerned, she told the constables. In the early hours of 13 August, though, a mysterious car drew up at their house. She remembered that it had a southern registration. Which county? She didn't notice that: only that it was white with the familiar blue EU emblem. There were two men. Her husband packed a small bag with clothes and left with them, taking £1000 in cash.

It was all a bit flimsy but as yet the Enniskillen police had no reason to suspect Julie of anything. Gerry McGinley was no stranger to them. He'd been arrested—not by them but by their colleagues over the border—two months earlier. A tip-off had led to the Gardaí in County Cavan arresting him at a border checkpoint. He was detained at Blacklion when they found drugs with a street value of several thousand pounds in the boot of his car. Gerry had vehemently denied his guilt, claiming that somebody had tried to frame him. After hours of wrangling with his solicitor the Guards released him, assuring him that it was unlikely he'd be prosecuted.

These facts were known to the RUC. Yet Julie was insisting that Gerry still feared prosecution. She suggested this as his reason for fleeing—for by this time she believed that her husband was on the run.

———

So far the police weren't treating the house in Ballinamallard as a crime scene. If the story Julie told of the two men from the Republic were true then Gerry had left of his own free will. Nevertheless they had to be sure that no foul play had taken place in the McGinley home.

One of the first things they noted was that the master bedroom, where the couple slept, was newly decorated. When, they asked, was this done? Two days after Gerry's disappearance, Julie told them. The carpet was dirty and could no longer be cleaned satisfactorily. She'd engaged their friend Pat McPadden to lay a new one. Eyebrows were raised, but she assured the investigators that all was above board. Gerry and she had already decorated most of the house; they'd planned this together but she'd finished the job in his absence; there was nothing to be read into it.

But the police weren't certain of that. A forensics team set to work and before long made an unusual find in the back garden. Somebody had been burning debris from the 'decorating'. They found what turned out to be the charred remains of a pair of jeans and what was clearly a man's watch. The rest of the burnt material seemed to be some sort of fabric.

They added this evidence to a piece of information gleaned from Julie's brother-in-law, Harry McGinley. The morning after Gerry's disappearance he'd seen Julie buying new bedclothes at a market in the town.

More inquiries were to produce information that was possibly relevant to the case. The McGinleys were in debt to the tune of £80,000. And Julie stood to collect £300,000 in the event of her husband's death.

He was not dead, though—and the RUC were ruling nothing out at this stage. The talk in the town was of a love affair that Mrs McGinley was conducting with her husband's business partner, Michael Monaghan, a married man. He was forty-two, similar in build to the missing man. In poor light he might even be mistaken for him—especially by a young babysitter, bleary-eyed at 2.30 am and having thoughts only for her warm bed.

It is widely held that in order for a person to be charged with murder a body must be produced, or the remains of one. This is not the case. Many of the greatest murder trials in history were successfully prosecuted on circumstantial evidence alone.

The RUC had three suspects: Julie McGinley, Michael Monaghan and Pat McPadden. All had opportunity, and the first two might have had a motive. If Julie and Michael were lovers then they might have wished for Gerry to be out of the way. There was one niggling problem, however. If Gerry's body were not recovered, the insurance company wouldn't pay out. She stood to forfeit £300,000. And she was still £80,000 in debt. Michael Monaghan would need to work very hard and very long to pay off her debt for her.

And so the investigation dragged on for six more months, the police finding very little concrete evidence. The forensics experts went to work again on the bedroom Julie shared with Gerry. They found semen stains on the mattress and had Michael Monaghan provide a sample of his own. They matched.

The RUC continued to interview witnesses in Enniskillen. Piece by piece they were building up a picture of Gerry McGinley's true activities. They heard how he'd boast of 'baiting' men in hotel rooms. Julie was the accomplice, the seducer. The venue was always the Fort Lodge Hotel, a small establishment in the shadow of one of Enniskillen's great landmarks: the Cole Monument, a column reminiscent of the Nelson memorial that once stood in Dublin's O'Connell Street.

Gerry McGinley was not a reader of books, yet he could not fail to have heard tell of Oscar Wilde, the most famous pupil at nearby Portora Royal School for boys. As a youngster Wilde passed many a pleasant hour in the gardens at the foot of the memorial, the gardens laid on the slopes of Fort Hill. Local legend has it that their beauty inspired one of his earlier children's stories, 'The Happy Prince'. On a calm summer's day in this historic town it's easy to think away the rumble of the traffic and see the young Oscar dreaming on the grass under a spreading oak, with the scent of wild roses on the air.

But the reader might remember too how Wilde met his downfall, and find in the McGinleys' activities in the Fort Lodge a striking parallel. In Wilde's day the rent boys of London had a lucrative sideline: blackmail. The unwary customer might find himself shopped to the peelers if he weren't careful, for in those days sodomy was a very serious criminal offence. Wilde was continually on his guard against this. It was a slip of the tongue that was his undoing when during his fateful trial he expressed his disgust at a certain rent boy's ugliness.

Gerry McGinley was in the habit of renting the same room in the Fort Lodge Hotel. None of the staff questioned this. It was assumed that he liked the view of Wilde's beloved park the room afforded him. In reality he had rigged up his video equipment here. It could be activated when a secret switch was pressed. This was Julie's job, and she hated it.

Down in the bar the pretty blonde would have propositioned a businessman or prosperous-looking farmer. No money would be involved, simply the promise of sex for nothing. It would be irresistible; few could turn her down. Once upstairs in the rented room Julie would ensure that the 'client' was videotaped in a compromising position, or two. They would pay up and shut up when sent a copy of the tape, and Gerry McGinley would profit.

But he spent the money as fast as he made it. He liked to live high on the hog. He liked to gamble too. Despite the blackmail, he sank deeper and deeper into debt.

He was also getting deeper into trouble. His list of enemies was growing longer with each blackmail threat. He came to be despised even by those who hadn't fallen victim to his schemes. No one likes a blackmailer. When told of Gerry's disappearance somebody remarked that it was good that 'that psychotic bastard will not be coming back'.

How did he know? He wasn't the only one who seemed convinced that Gerry had met his end. Michael Monaghan had been a little too loose of tongue with a certain Josephine McElroy, known to her friends as Lulu. Prior to August he'd intimated to Lulu that Gerry's days were numbered. He'd spoken of a man named Tony McNern who was 'going to get McGinley sorted out'. Should that fail, he'd hinted darkly, he himself would have to get somebody to 'sort him out'. The truth emerged: even Monaghan had fallen for McGinley's blackmail trap and had tendered £20,000. It was a good reason to hate one's business partner.

The RUC were looking ever more closely into Michael Monaghan's private affairs. Julie was continuing to deny that she was having an affair with him. Their breakthrough came when they discovered portions of a love-letter in Michael's van. They were in a notebook and barely legible; they'd been scribbled over. It didn't take long, though, for a handwriting expert to decipher them. Both were addressed to 'Julie'.

One read that 'there's not a minute of every day that goes by that you're not in my mind'. The other spoke of love several times. It included the enigmatic lines: 'If anything happens to me or goes wrong don't worry' and 'if there's anything you need or want to talk about all you have to do is phone and I will be there.'

People had seen Julie and Michael together, on more than one occasion engaging in sex in one or the other's car. The affair was a poorly kept secret. Inevitably Michael's wife Patricia found out—and slapped Julie's face in public for her pains.

All evidence pointed to two prime suspects, Julie and Michael, and a minor role played by Pat McPadden. The police moved on 24 March 2001 and took all three into custody.

Detective Inspector Brian McArthur admitted that although no body had been found he had 'overwhelming circumstantial evidence' that one or all was guilty.

Then they found the body.

––––

On 4 June 2001 a girl of nine was out walking with her mother, two sisters and an aunt near the town of Ballinamore in County Leitrim. It lies almost due south of Enniskillen; if a motorist were to cross into the Twenty-Six Counties at Swanlinbar, Ballinamore would be the first town of any size encountered. The area is one of outstanding beauty, heather-mantled rolling countryside, with Lough Erne to the east and the Iron Mountains to the west.

The girl rambled off the path the three were following, and came upon a gruesome sight. The flies and the overpowering stench should have warned her, but nothing could have prepared her for the bones. They were white, picked clean by birds and carrion creatures. They were sticking up out of the earth, and there were many more attached. Little flesh remained on them; there was not much left of Gerry McGinley's body, having lain for ten months in the ground.

DNA tests carried out by Dr Marie Cassidy, the state pathologist, confirmed the identity of the corpse in the shallow grave. She noted that the skull had been struck at least three times. The force of one blow had been so strong that the brain was detached and sent careering into the far side of the skull, fracturing it on both sides. Gerry's head would have been split open and blood spattered everywhere. Had he been attacked in his sleep, Dr Cassidy concluded, the bedclothes, the carpet and the walls of the bedroom would be stained considerably.

It would have been necessary to redecorate such a room.

The body could not be immediately identified for a simple enough reason; the killers had removed all the clothing and personal effects. The pathologist suggested that this measure had been taken to conceal the man's identity.

The killers were already in custody—of that the police were certain. Julie McGinley was denied bail. And for good reason. Since the time of the murder, she'd moved across the border to the Republic, and out of the jurisdiction of the RUC. More ominous was the fact that she'd applied for Australian citizenship. There was a very real possibility that she'd make a run for it.

The police were satisfied that they could obtain a conviction. The body was there and, while the evidence was still largely circumstantial, it pointed to Julie's participation in the murder. When the case came before the Belfast Crown Court in April 2001, however, the prosecutor was mocked for the quality of his witnesses. The three key witnesses were so poor and unreliable that the defending barrister referred to them scathingly as 'a drunken criminal', 'a rogue' and 'a snake in the grass'.

The drunkard was Lulu McElroy. It was shown that she'd no fewer than forty-four criminal convictions on her record sheet, many committed while she was highly inebriated.

'You have to ask yourself just how reliable this woman is,' he told the jury, 'or whether you would happily convict a man of murder on the word of a woman like that.'

The 'rogue' was one Patrick Owens, a man who repeatedly refused to answer questions put to him by the defence. He seemed to have it in for Michael Monaghan.

'I say to you that the man is simply a rogue,' contended Julie's counsel. 'Not only that, he is a rogue with a motive to harm Mr Monaghan—because he feels that Mr Monaghan is in some way responsible for him losing a lot of money.'

The 'snake in the grass' was Robert Elliot, the neighbour who'd reported Gerry's disappearance to the RUC, according to the defence lawyer. He was 'a prime example of how the most surprising things in a criminal case lie under the surface'.

'Who would have guessed,' Julie's counsel went on, 'that this good neighbour of the McGinleys was the person who, behind all the scenes, was stirring it up?'

He was alluding to bizarre acts on Elliot's part. The neighbour had sent Christmas and Valentine's Day cards to another neighbour of Julie's, pretending they'd come from her, and vice versa.

However, the defence didn't get its own way for long. Day by day, as the trial went into its second week, then its third—and finally its thirteenth—the evidence was stacking up against the three.

There was no denying that Julie had redecorated the bedroom with undue haste. And Pat McPadden had laid the carpet. It was moreover shown that McPadden came from Ballinamore, precisely where the body was found.

They had burned the dead man's clothes in the backyard. They even tried to dispose of his watch—a watch that was a present from his own children. Julie had no intention of reporting his disappearance either.

But perhaps what damned the accused most was a remark Michael Monaghan made to Patrick Owens shortly after the disappearance. Gerry McGinley, he suggested callously, was 'probably pushing up heather on some mountain'. It was so close to the actual circumstances that the jury members caught their collective breath. They were ready to convict.

McPadden was found not guilty, there being insufficient evidence to charge him with anything bar his friendship with the others. Both Julie and Michael got the same tariff: fifteen years behind bars. They will not be due for parole for some time.

In some respects the case bore a resemblance to the Gault murder, committed in Lisburn three months earlier. Like Paul Gault, Gerry McGinley was slain in his own bedroom and by his wife's lover. But Lesley Ann Gault was freed from Maghaberry Prison in County Antrim when her innocence was at last proven on 8 October 2004.

The difference was that Gerry hadn't put up a struggle of any kind. He couldn't—he was fast asleep. Mr Justice Kerr, when passing sentence on both, described the murder as an 'opportunist killing' and 'callous and chilling'.

No weapon was ever found.

DOLORES O'NEILL, THE WIFE WHO WALKED INTO DOORS

There is nothing out of the ordinary or even vaguely sinister about Coolamber Park, Knocklyon. It's everything the resident of a two-up, two-down corporation house in nearby Tallaght aspires to: leafy, secluded and quiet. It's expensive too, its homes costing more than the average first-time mortgage borrower can manage. Small wonder then that most of the residents of this community to the south of Dublin city are middle aged with grown-up children. The real wonder is that Coolamber was the scene of two domestic killings in recent years. Chip-shop owner Franco Sacco died there in 1997, gunned down by a fifteen-year-old girl. On 22 July 2002 Declan O'Neill met a gruesome end a few doors away, at number 45. His death was also by a female hand: that of his wife Dolores.

If a name given at christening can influence a child's future then that given to Dolores could hardly have been more appropriate. In Latin it means 'sorrows' and this woman was to have plenty.

If we're to believe her—and let us do so in the absence of any evidence to the contrary—her sorrows began two weeks before her wedding day. Declan struck her. Although he'd been drinking it was nevertheless a cowardly act. He was six feet tall; she barely came up to his shoulder.

That first assault was to set a pattern for the years to follow. Dolores should have cancelled the wedding there and then but didn't.

What would people think?

It was well that the 'people' didn't accompany them when the couple honeymooned in Greece, because once again Declan gave a disquieting demonstration of the sort of man he was. Again he had too much to drink, picked a fight—and tried to throttle his bride on the balcony of their hotel. Dolores had looked forward to the honeymoon as any newlyweds would: two weeks of married bliss before settling down to the serious business of spending the rest of one's life together. Declan saw the honeymoon through other eyes.

'I suppose it was an excuse to be drinking during the day,' Dolores was to say later.

By her account, though, Declan O'Neill needed no excuse. If it wasn't obvious before it soon became clear to Dolores: she'd married an alcoholic. To be sure, statistically speaking one in every five Irishmen is either an alcoholic or has a serious drink problem. And as if that weren't enough, her husband was a man who liked to be in control of others, to have others at his beck and call. He was a skilled labourer, a tradesman who dreamed one day of having his own business. The longer he worked for another, the longer that dream was denied him, the greater became his need to domineer. Unfortunately for Dolores she was not an assertive person; Declan could impose his will on her whenever he wished. And that is exactly what he did.

She worked as a civil servant, attached to the Legal Aid Board, and in time joined the Equality Authority. This arrangement didn't suit Declan, though; he preferred any wife of his to be housebound, to be there when he got home.

'He loved the idea of coming in and having his meals on the table and the fire lit,' Dolores remembers.

In that respect he was very traditional. In other ways he was not. He liked music. He collected old guitars and old vinyl records, and composed his own pop songs, though nothing ever came of them. This was the gentle, sensitive side of Declan O'Neill.

When Dolores was pregnant with her first child, Brian, in 1978, she took leave of absence but returned to work soon after the birth. Declan wasn't happy with this, even though a relative was looking after the baby.

He wanted to eat his cake and have it too, however. They soon discovered it was tough going with only Declan's wages coming in. She either had to return to work or the family had to economize. Declan was not prepared to live in reduced circumstances. In fact he was working hard to better himself. The move to Coolamber Park in prestigious Knocklyon was part of this upward mobility.

His drinking appears to have increased alarmingly at this point. Certainly when a second son was born in 1986 it was so out of control that the family were suffering. Dolores recollects writing a cheque for £25 that bounced, causing her intense embarrassment. In order to make ends meet she took a job selling mass cards in the evenings and at weekends. It paid only £2 an hour but if they were careful they could manage. The bills had to be paid out of her account.

She dared not complain, even when he was making her life a misery. He would abuse her both verbally and physically. She rarely saw him any more.

'He'd go off on a Thursday when he got paid,' she recalls, 'and we wouldn't see him until Saturday.'

His moods became dark and violent. Once he even threatened her life.

'I'm mixing with people now who can make people disappear,' he said. She didn't know what to make of that.

One Saturday morning when he was lying in bed still drunk from the night before she asked him for money for groceries. All she found of his weekly wage was £20 and some small change. She asked him where the rest was and he accused her of taking it.

They were continually running short of money because of Declan's drinking. Bills remained unpaid. The ESB cut off the power several times, and the phone company disconnected them on one or two occasions. As the years passed and her marriage spiralled steadily downwards, Declan became impossible to live with. She considered at one stage keeping him from the house, taking out a barring order against him. But she couldn't in the end.

What would people think?

———

At about one in the morning on 23 July 2002 Ann Hughes woke to the sound of the doorbell ringing. The light was already visible in the eastern sky above the little town of Ashford.

Ann found her sister Dolores on the doorstep, ashen-faced and nervous. She had her sons with her: Brian was now twenty-one, Conor was fifteen. Dolores asked her to 'look after them' while she had a word with Ann's husband John.

What she had to say shocked her brother-in-law so much that he could scarcely believe it. He stared at this diminutive woman with the mop of grey hair and kindly though perpetually troubled eyes. She appeared to be, in his own words, 'out of it, totally devastated and in a horrific state'. He noticed that her face was badly bruised but this did not surprise him; he was aware that Dolores had lived for many years—for more than two decades—in an abusive relationship. From what he could gather, when he had at last calmed her down, the relationship was over. Dolores had ended it in the most brutal way possible.

'I've done a terrible thing to the father of my sons,' she wailed.

As the story unfolded John was coming to appreciate just how terrible it was—though it's unlikely that he was aware of the full horror of Dolores's deed. Dolores could only tell him that she'd attacked Declan and that she 'must have been mad'.

Any sane person confronted with the corpse of her husband might have reached the same conclusion. Few would believe that a woman could be capable of such savagery—and certainly not a woman of Dolores's physical stature, character and temperament. For Declan's head and face had been battered almost beyond recognition, his throat stabbed so many times that it resembled a single, dreadful wound. Ceiling and walls—even the wall farthest from the bed—were spattered with Declan's blood; the bedding and mattress were soaked with it.

In fact 'every accessible surface' had blood on it, according to Garda David Connolly, who was first on the scene. He'd taken a phone call from a very agitated John Hughes. Dolores had been so incoherent that nobody could be sure whether or not Declan was dead. Guard Connolly's first sight of the bedroom confirmed it. In order to examine the corpse he'd had to step gingerly around a mass of bloodstains on the carpet. He found a carving knife lying on the bed next to the body. He was initially curious as to how the weapon could have done so much damage to Declan's skull, until he discovered a plumber's hammer on the soap tray in the en-suite bathroom; it was stained with blood.

Leaving everything as they found it, Connolly and a colleague went to the address in Ashford that Hughes had given them. Ann Hughes was upstairs in a bedroom, trying to calm her sister. Dolores was in no condition to make a statement. Her words were unintelligible as she rocked back and forth on the bed. The Guards brought her to the station.

Some hours later she confessed to attacking her husband. It was self-defence, she said, and ugly bruising to her face reinforced her story: that Declan had been banging her head against a wall while gripping her by the throat. However, the sight of the battered corpse in Coolamber Park was still very fresh in the Guards' mind and it was difficult to reconcile the two. Declan's death was the result of prolonged battering and stabbing. It went far beyond self-defence. They charged her with murder.

———

At her trial in 2004 Dolores traced the final months of her life with Declan O'Neill, but it was her sons Brian and Conor who provided judge, jury and public with the most disturbing picture of their mother's struggle.

Brian, a physics student, spoke of his father's drinking as a constant feature of his growing up. By July 2002 it was out of control.

'He couldn't continue much longer the way he was,' the twenty-three-year-old said.

Brian told how the atmosphere in the home changed whenever his father was about. At times he had to break up serious rows between his parents. He spoke of 'a constant state of tension in the house' and how he preferred to keep out of Declan's way.

He knew that his father was battering his mother, and refused to believe her when she tried to explain away her frequent bruises and cuts as accidents. The final straw was when she told him the cause of a severe bruise to her face on 22 July 2002. His father, she said, had accidentally opened a door on her.

That evening he and his younger brother Conor had gone to the cinema, leaving the parents alone together. The boys returned at about 11.40 pm to find Dolores sitting in their father's car outside the house. She was very distraught. She told them to get in and they drove away.

'Where are we going, Mum?' Brian asked.

He had to ask her a number of times because she seemed not to hear him. Finally she told her sons that they were on their way to her sister Ann's home in Ashford, County Wicklow.

'Is Dad okay?'

She wouldn't answer. Brian felt certain that his father had abused her yet again. She denied it, kept saying 'no'.

Not for a moment did he consider the possibility that Dolores had assaulted his father. It was unthinkable. She was never a violent person, always treating her sons with love and kindness. She never raised a hand to them.

'When I was younger,' he said, 'she used to lecture other parents on not hitting their children.'

What, then, had induced a quiet, gentle fifty-year-old mother to so brutally attack her husband? Why did she persist with her hammer blows and knife thrusts when two or three would have caused Declan's death? Brian's younger brother Conor recounted the events leading up to the tragedy.

He told the court that several months before he died, Declan had moved out of the family home. He knew that his father was living with another woman but his mother never alluded to this. Eventually Declan moved back to Coolamber Park towards the end of June. A few weeks later he suggested that Dolores and Conor accompany him to Cork; they would have a weekend together.

Conor sensed that nothing had changed when on their last night in the hotel he heard 'a loud bang' from his parents' room. The following morning at breakfast Dolores was displaying a badly bruised face. It was 21 July 2002, the day before the killing.

Nor could Dolores's colleagues and supervisors explain the seeming transformation that occurred. According to Frank Brady, assistant chief officer with the Legal Aid Board, she was an excellent, hard-working employee. Brian Merriman, head of communications with the Equality Authority, backed him up. Dolores, he said, was an asset to the organization, particularly good with young people, always showing kindness and patience.

He sensed, however, that there had been 'personal difficulties'; there'd been extended leaves of absence from work. But she was reluctant to discuss her affairs; she was what he called 'a very private person'. What raised suspicion among her colleagues was the fact that Dolores always appeared in the office with arms and neck fully covered, no matter what the weather.

Sandra Cavanagh, her supervisor, was also full of praise for Dolores, both as an employee and as an individual. She described her as 'a very quiet, gentle person, whose voice was never raised'. It seems that everybody thought very highly of her.

The court was no further to discovering why Dolores had behaved as she did. Only when the defendant herself appeared in the witness box did the true nature of her relationship with Declan emerge. Her testimony was a litany of drunkenness, beatings, verbal abuse, domineering and callous disregard for her feelings.

Towards the end, she said, Declan's bouts of rage had become so violent that she had to lie about the nature of her injuries. She remembered one particular assault when he punched her in the face. She didn't know her nose was bleeding until her son Brian drew her attention to it.

'It was always very tense when Declan was in the house,' she said. 'You could cut the air with a knife.'

Dolores corroborated her son's testimony that Declan had moved out of the house a few months before he died. The court was shocked to hear that the woman he'd shacked up with was a dominatrix. Evidently the domineering Declan needed a strong woman to take control of him. Dolores was hardly that. Was this why he despised her?

And to judge from her testimony he did indeed have utter contempt for her. He knew when he'd moved out that Dolores would have difficulty running the home alone. She had to resort to phoning him on a Wednesday, the day before payday.

'What are you at me for now?' he'd ask angrily. 'Why are you phoning me?' She had to explain that there was no heating in the house, bills were left unpaid and the mortgage was in arrears.

'I'd have to meet him in a pub,' she told the court, 'and he'd throw money at me.'

Eventually she persuaded him to move back. The trip to Cork was her way of attempting a reconciliation: 'I just wanted to try one last time to make it as a family.'

The journey to Cork did not augur well for the success of this last-ditch attempt. It was as tense as any car journey Dolores had experienced with her husband. He resented the CDs she'd brought along for the trip and wore earplugs rather than listen to them.

But that night in the hotel she imagined there was hope yet. She woke up with Declan kissing her. The hope was short lived. When she kissed his shoulder in reciprocation he recoiled from her in rage.

'You fucking bitch!' he roared. 'Are you trying to leave your mark on me or what?'

She was confused.

'What's going on?' she asked.

His response was to hit her with his fist. She spent the remainder of the night in the bathroom, a damp flannel pressed to her face to bring down the swelling. On the return journey to Dublin she sat in the back seat with Conor, trying to hide her injury from him. She phoned in sick the next morning, rather than face awkward enquiries. Brian was appalled by the black eye and bruising and suggested she go and see a doctor, that he might photograph the evidence while it was still fresh.

She must have known that day that any hope of leading a normal life with her husband was doomed to failure. It was perhaps that day, while she was nursing her swollen face and her emotional heartache, that she vowed to put an end to her suffering. She would not contemplate any such action while her sons were about, of course. She loved the boys so dearly that the thought of hurting them unnecessarily was anathema to her.

But Dolores swore in the courtroom, on the Bible and in front of judge and jury, that she planned nothing. Declan it was who drove her to it. She acted only out of self-preservation.

Declan, for his part, played right into her hands that evening. She hadn't had time to do any shopping before the Cork trip and consequently there was not much food in the house. But she made do with what she had, putting together an ample dinner. She placed Declan's food on a tray and took it up to him. He was surly. Later she brought him a cup of tea.

'What the fuck are you in here again for?' he demanded.

Later she asked to borrow his car to bring the boys to the cinema. Declan lost his rag.

'Jesus Christ!' he shouted. 'You're in on top of me again. What the fucking hell is wrong with your own car?'

'I'm low on petrol.'

'Get me some fags then in that case,' he said, flinging the keys at her. She retreated.

With Brian and Conor safely away she returned with his car keys and the cigarettes. Again he shouted at her.

'I didn't move back home for you to be in on top of me,' he said.

When she brought him more tea he ordered her out. It was plain that he couldn't bear to have her around him. So much for trying again 'one last time'.

She knew he'd reached breaking point when she had to disturb him yet again. She was putting on a wash and went to his room to gather up his dirty laundry. That was when he jumped up from the bed.

'He started calling me "a fucking bitch"', Dolores told the court. 'He pushed me up against a table.'

He grabbed her by the throat and forced her up against the wall. He banged her head again and again on the wall. She couldn't breathe, feeling his grip tightening about her throat. And all the while he was shouting, spitting in her face and threatening to give her a black eye to match the first.

Somehow she managed to free herself and push him away from her. He tumbled back onto the bed; she lost her balance and fell to the floor. It was then she saw a large plumber's hammer under the bed where Declan had shoved it for the time being. He'd been doing some DIY.

'I just saw the hammer and picked it up,' she said. She broke down. 'Oh Jesus! Oh God Jesus!'

She was remembering the slaughter.

———

The defence barrister, Felix McEnroy SC, would try to show that Dolores's version of events was the true one. Unfortunately the prosecutor's evidence indicated no resistance on Declan's part. It seemed more than a probability that he was either asleep 'or disabled by the first blow'. There were no 'defensive injuries': marks or scratches on Declan that would indicate a struggle. He'd put up no resistance.

The toxicology report also showed not a trace of alcohol in Declan's blood, apparently contradicting his sons' and wife's contention that he had a serious drink problem.

The simple explanation seemed to be that Dolores, with malice aforethought, had entered Declan's room while he was sleeping—and done him to death with excessive force. Multiple blows of a hammer and multiple stab wounds could hardly be considered a reasonable response to an assault by an unarmed man.

The jury after much deliberation found her guilty of manslaughter.

There was no question of madness—even temporary insanity. Dolores, according to Justice Paul Carney, had slaughtered her husband when in the full possession of her faculties.

He was upset that the character of the deceased had been brought into the case—though in fairness it's hard to see how a defence could have been mounted without doing so. With great regret, for Dolores was 'clearly a good mother and is devoted to her two boys', he sentenced her to eight years in prison.

———

In the end the case hinged on one vital question: Did Declan put up a struggle or not; was Dolores acting in self-defence?

I'm inclined to the view taken by many that the victim was asleep when the attack took place. Much was made of the fact that no 'defensive wounds' were found on his arms and hands. Dolores stuck doggedly to her story that it was Declan who made the assault on her and she was simply defending herself. She pushed Declan, he fell backwards onto the bed, she picked up a hammer and hit him several times. At some point she blacked out and could not recall the later stages of the attack, in particular her use of the knife.

I have immense difficulty with this version of events. The killing took place in Declan's bedroom. Dolores stated that when her husband fell onto the bed she happened to see a hammer lying under it, picked it up and used it. While I find it unlikely, I can accept that this is indeed possible. But the carving knife? Did Dolores have it about her person? How do you conceal a carving knife? Was she holding it when she entered the bedroom? In that case Declan's alleged attack on her could only be construed as self-defence on his part.

The media made much of the pathologist's report, which stated that Declan had been struck repeatedly from above. He was therefore supine when each if not all of the blows fell. It was inferred by one journalist that Dolores 'had straddled her sleeping husband in bed before bludgeoning him to death'.

This is an appalling mental picture. The image thus conjured up has both sexual and sadistic overtones. It is highly emotive. It's an image of a she-devil or succubus, said to ravish men in their sleep. It's also an image of a crazed she-warrior clubbing her helpless victim to death—while remaining in total control.

I cannot accept this inference. It hardly accords at all with the picture Dolores's boys painted of their mother. Nor do I believe that the state pathologist implied any such thing. To be sure, she stated that the attack was from above, and her predecessor Professor Harbison—retired but asked for his opinion—agreed. But the fact is that any attack on a prone or supine man will always be from above. One doesn't need to *straddle* that man. A woman of Dolores's size need only lean over the man and strike. Moreover, the pathologist reported wounds to the right of the head, and this is consistent with an attacker standing to one side of the bed. Even if Declan were sleeping, Dolores would hardly have risked climbing onto the bed and straddling him; he might easily have woken up and overpowered her before she had a chance to deal the first blow of the hammer.

I believe that Declan was indeed asleep on the night of 22 July 2002. Exactly when she decided to kill him is a moot point but I'm inclined to think it was soon after the boys had left the house to go to the cinema. She must have been smarting still—both mentally and physically—from the beating Declan had given her in Cork.

She probably did go to his room to fetch some laundry. On finding him asleep, or snoozing, after a heavy meal and a cup of tea, she might have quietly left the room, fearing a repeat of his earlier bad-tempered outburst. She might have made up her mind at that moment to be rid of him once and for all.

I believe that only a short time elapsed between her making her mind up and carrying out the attack. Her sons were safely out of the way. She'd never have dreamt of killing their father in their presence; it would have been unthinkable.

I don't believe she found the hammer under the bed. It was too convenient. More likely that she chose her weapon with care from Declan's toolbox, or that the hammer was lying elsewhere in the house—in the kitchen or a bathroom; it was a plumber's hammer after all; it would have been close to plumbing.

She might have chosen two weapons, to make sure. The hammer was heavy, her hands were shaking; there was every possibility that she'd drop it, thereby waking Declan. He'd surely do her tremendous damage were he to think she was going to attack him with it. He might even kill her. So she took the knife along as an alternative.

I don't believe that she consciously set out to bludgeon him twenty-four times, or stab him more than twenty times. I'm inclined to think that she approached his bed with the hammer, trembling with fear, and struck once.

The blow, to the temple, the cheek or the eye-socket, would not have killed him. He either awoke briefly or was stunned, and groaned. In either case he was still alive. Dolores would have known that her own life was in danger. She would have been in a blue funk—and fear is the key.

I think it was fear that drove her to rain down as many blows as she could, to make certain that Declan would not rise again to attack her. The man was far more powerful than she was; he'd proved this time and again. She dared not allow him to get up again to assault her. And so she kept going, in a fear-induced frenzy. The sight of his blood would have been enough to cause this mild little woman to become temporarily unhinged. She probably blacked out after the third or fourth blow was struck. She stated that she'd no recollection of going downstairs to get the knife. Why would she, if Declan were clearly already very dead? I think she had both weapons to hand, and used both either simultaneously or one after the other.

She changed her clothing and washed off the blood. What woman would not? It must be most distressing to have your dead husband's blood on your body. Nor could she remain in that house. The thought of what she'd done and the memory of the bloodied corpse on the bed would have been altogether too much to bear. She'd have wanted to get a million miles away from there but knew that her sons were returning that same night. She must have been in such turmoil as she waited in the dark, alone, in her car.

Finally, I'm of the opinion that her sentence was excessive. I don't think she deserved eight years in prison. Certainly not when she was provoked beyond endurance. It might be argued that provocation as a defence should only be used when a person kills in the heat of the moment, when his or her life is threatened. Yet Dolores's life was continually under threat, and her provocation was cumulative. It seems that it was only a matter of time before Declan killed her. The statistics show that an abusive husband is likely to kill his wife in the end. In this respect the male is far more deadly than the female.

She should have sought another way out of her tormented situation. And there is always a way. She could have confided in more people than she did; even her sons were fed the lie that she 'walked into a door'. Too many women in Dolores's situation are reluctant to seek help, often because they fear their husband's wrath should he find out. This is a well-founded fear. Yet women's shelters deal with cases of battered wives every day, and there is always a solution, though it might not be apparent at the time.

The worst excuse for not exposing an abusive husband is, 'What will people think?' In fact most people will not think badly of the 'tattletale' but of the abuser—other women especially, given the prevalence in our society of this sustained attack upon the weaker partner in a relationship.

All decent, principled men must surely recoil from it too—and treat such cowardice with the contempt it deserves.

Also by David M Kiely

Murder by a female hand can be just as brutal as by a male. *Bloody Women* contains drownings, shootings, stabbings and savage clubbings, as well as highlighting the ingenious methods by which some of Ireland's female killers disposed of their victim's corpse.

Here are women who murdered their lovers; or who murdered relations in dispute over land and inheritance. Jane O'Brien from County Wexford who shot her own nephew in order to get possession of a farm; and Hannah O'Leary who killed and dismembered one of her older brothers in County Cork. Here too is Mamie Cadden, the Hume Street abortionist.

Bloody Women tells the stories of seventeen Irish murders, all committed by women. Some are notorious, some less well known: all reveal that the dark forces which drive men to murder are fully shared by women.

By Barry Cummins

Among the cases in *Lifers* is Ireland's longest serving prisoner, an inmate for over forty years who refuses to apply for parole. Also profiled are random killers John Shaw and Geoffrey Evans, who abducted and murdered women in Counties Wicklow and Mayo in 1976. Then there is the twenty-three-year investigation into the murder of Kildare woman Phyllis Murphy which saw John Crerar jailed for life in 2002.

As well as an in-depth look at how some of Ireland's most evil killers were caught, *Lifers* highlights issues that the criminal justice system must address. Barry Cummins argues that it is the families of murder victims who are the people really serving a life sentence. This is a riveting book that raises matters of profound public concern.

By Gene Kerrigan

Hard Cases is a collection of startling stories about the reality of crime and court cases in Ireland. In these stories, there are no crime bosses with quaint nicknames; the police don't collect convenient clues that tell them who dunnit. Instead, we get cases both famous and obscure in which the outcome is sometimes just, sometimes unsettling.

It begins with 'Dessie O'Hare's Last Stand', which records in breathtaking detail the inside story of a notorious kidnapping. It ends with 'The Small Legend of Karl Crawley', the story of a sometimes gentle, sometimes wild young Dublin man who found a shocking way of fighting back against authority.

Drugs, violence, robbery, murder and incest – Gene Kerrigan tells the big stories of twenty years of crime in Ireland. Written in his addictive style, once you've started reading, you won't be able to stop.

By Tom Reddy

Murder Will Out

Murder Will Out tells the story of ten sensational Irish
murders and how they were solved. The emphasis
throughout the book is on the work of the Gardaí,
concentrating on the painstaking and patient work that
led to successful prosecutions of the accused.
Every case detailed resulted in a conviction.

The Murder File

For twenty years, George Lawlor was head of the Murder
Squad in Ireland. A remarkable detective by any standard, his
work resulted in the Gardaí having one of the highest murder
detection rates in the world during his time in charge. Tautly
written, this is a collection of his cases, including murders
done for love, money and jealousy. Compulsive reading!